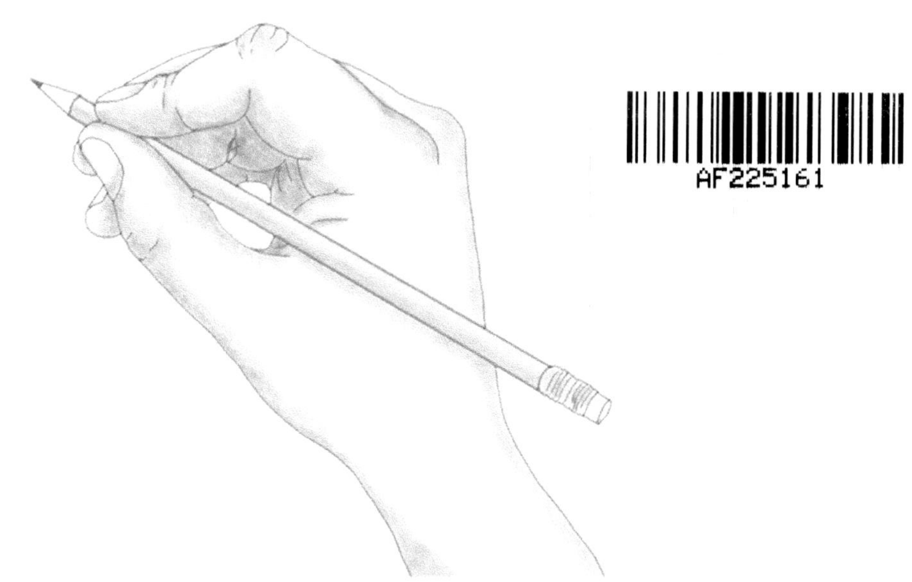

How to Draw

Flowers

Step-by-Step Botanical

Drawing Projects

Alisa Calder

Drawing 101

Have you always wanted to learn to draw but didn't know where to start? Learning to draw can seem overwhelming, but by using the step-by-step method you will soon be drawing better than you thought possible.

This book contains tutorials that will teach you how to draw many types of flowers and plants. Each step-by-step tutorial will guide you from the first step to the finished drawing.

Each diagram on the left shows you how to draw the object one step at a time. Simply follow along drawing in the space provided on the right-hand side. Add each detail as shown until the picture is finished.

Start off drawing lightly and don't worry about making mistakes. You can always erase and start over.

When you're finished, you can add your own details and color if you wish.

How to Draw Flowers: Step-by-Step Botanical Drawing Projects is perfect for beginners who want to quickly gain a sense of mastery in their drawing. Suitable for children, teens, and adults who want to practice and improve their drawing skills.

Tools for Drawing

When getting started drawing, there are a few basic tools and materials needed.

PENCILS

Buying a couple of quality drawing pencils will help you achieve the best results. Pencils come in a wide variety of materials, hardness, and colors. They are rated using a scale from 9B (softest and darkest) to 9H (hardest and lightest). For most purposes you will want to use the following types of pencils:

HB pencils – These are nice middle-ground pencils, neither too hard nor too soft. They are good for light line drawings and erase well. While limited in toning and shading capabilities, they are good for a beginner. These are equivalent to a standard #2 pencil.

2B pencils – These are on the harder end of the range. They make good general drawing pencils, can be smudged, and erase easily.

4B pencils – These types of pencils are softer than 2B and are good for sketching.

6B pencils – These pencils are good for shading and adding in darker tones to a sketch. Good blending and smudging. Softer, so will not last as long as HB and 2B pencils.

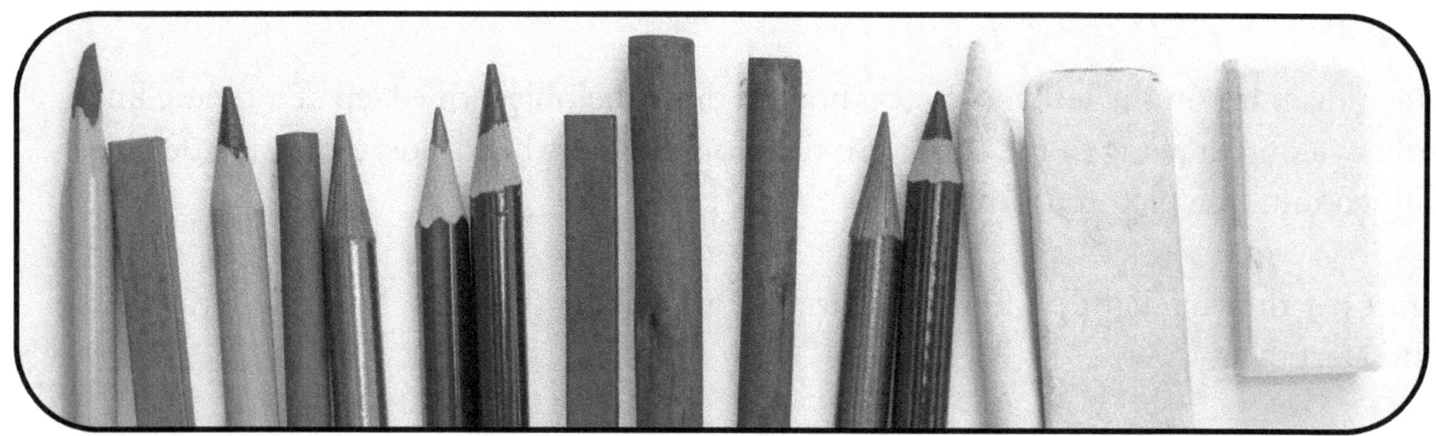

ERASERS

Mistakes are a part of life and thankfully we have erasers! Erasers can also be used to make different marks on paper. There are several types of erasers including rubber, kneaded, gum, and plastic. Have a couple of types on hand.

PAPER

Paper quality is an important component of a drawing. The texture (or tooth) and weight of the paper affect how much drawing material is left on the paper and the look of the finished drawing. Standard drawing paper has a medium texture and is suitable for most projects.

PENCIL SHARPENER

A quality pencil sharpener is needed to keep pencils sharp.

These are the basic tools needed by anyone interested in drawing. As you advance, there are other tools you may wish to acquire such as charcoal, ink pens, colored pencils, and blending stumps.

The tutorials on the following pages will walk you through drawing many types of plants, flowers, fruits, and vegetables. By the end of the book you should have the skills and confidence to create your own unique works of art.

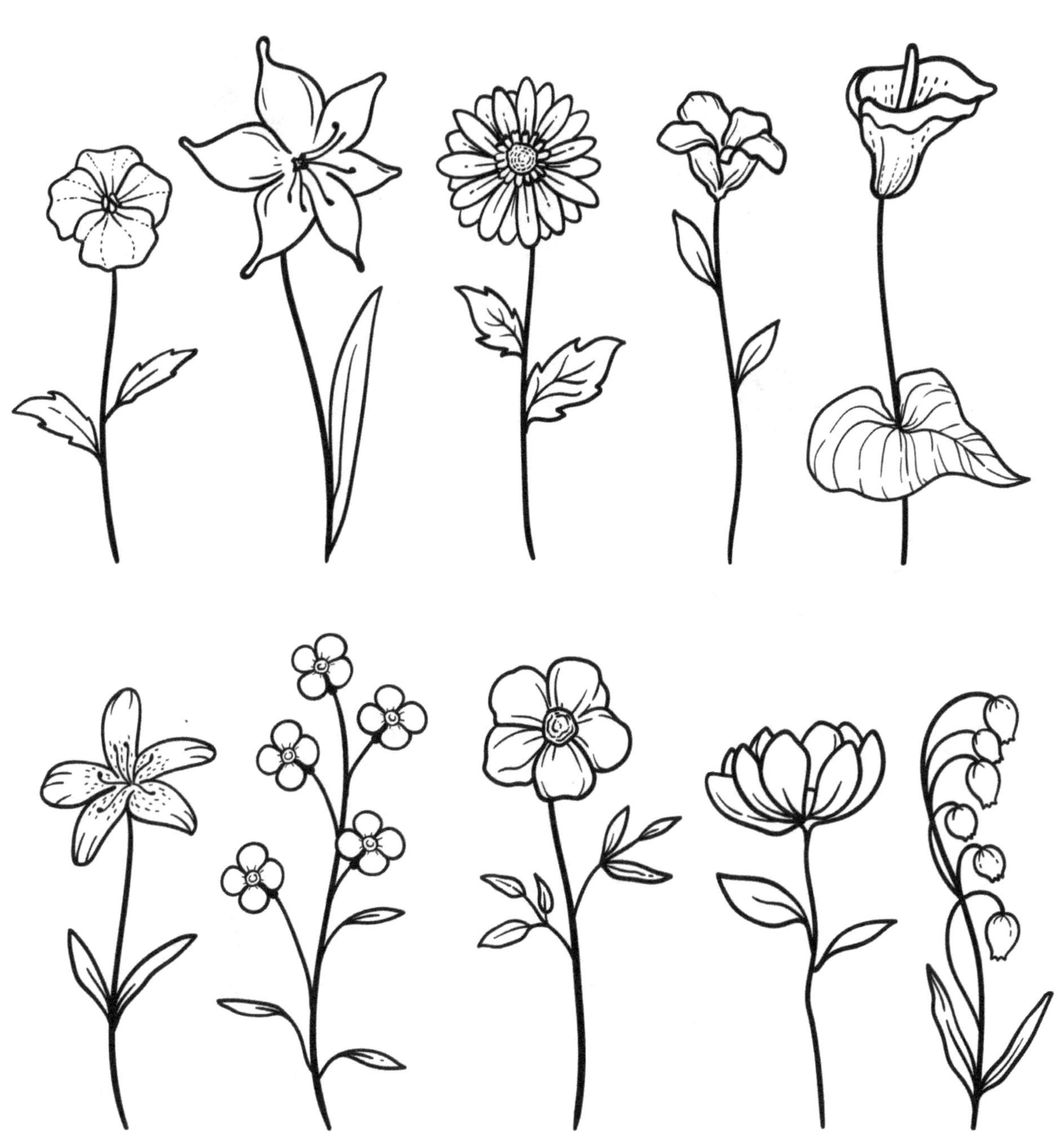

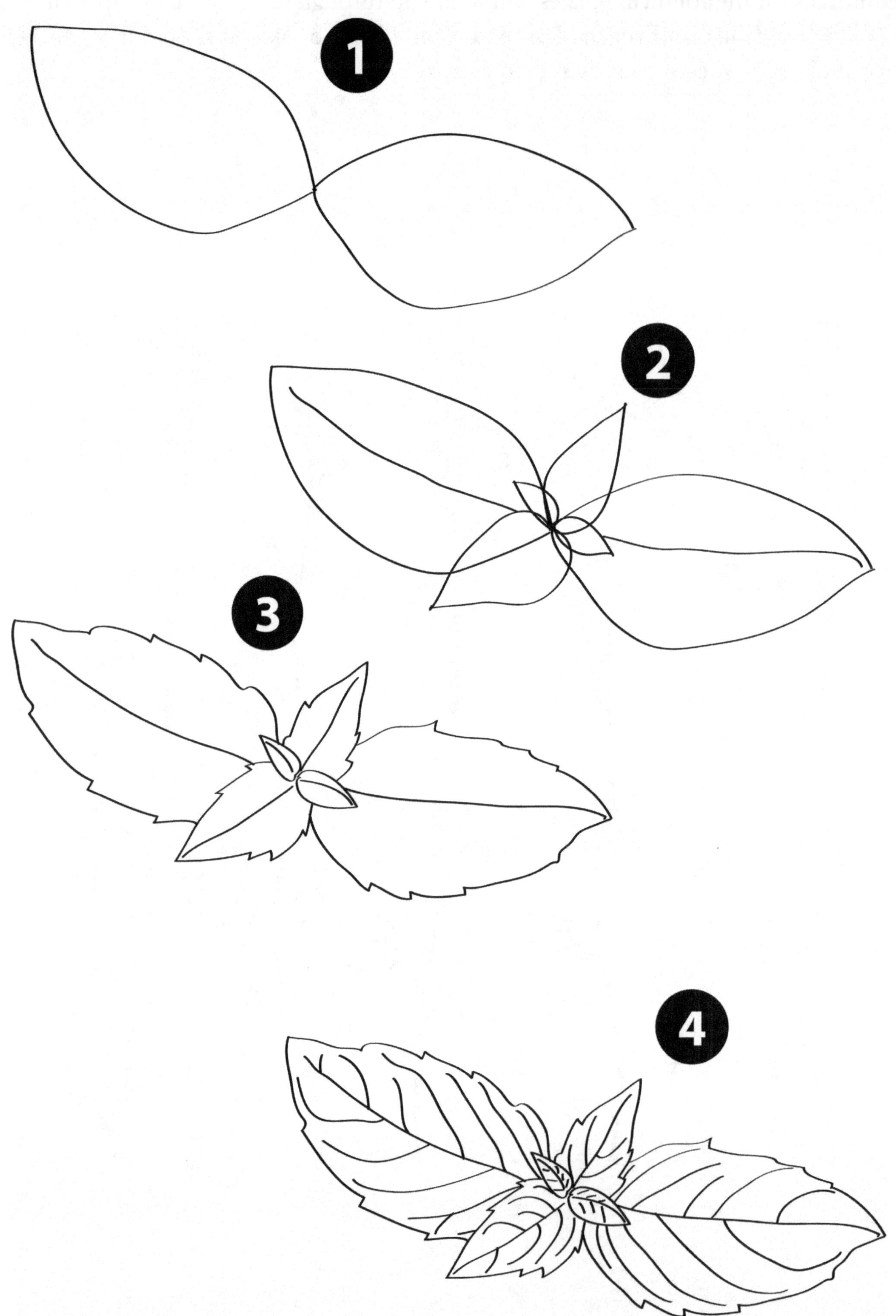

Your Turn to Draw

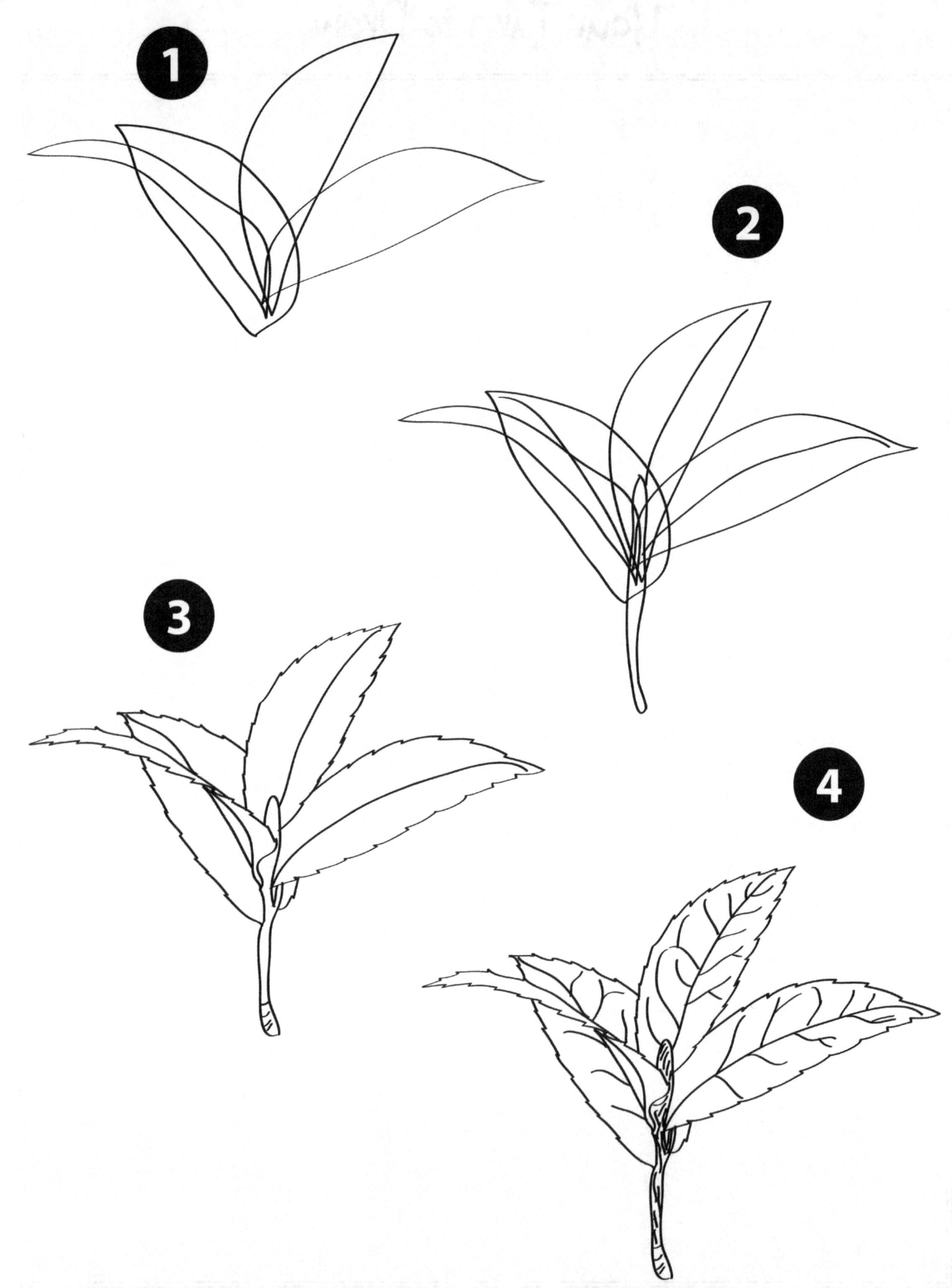

1
2
3
4

Your Turn to Draw

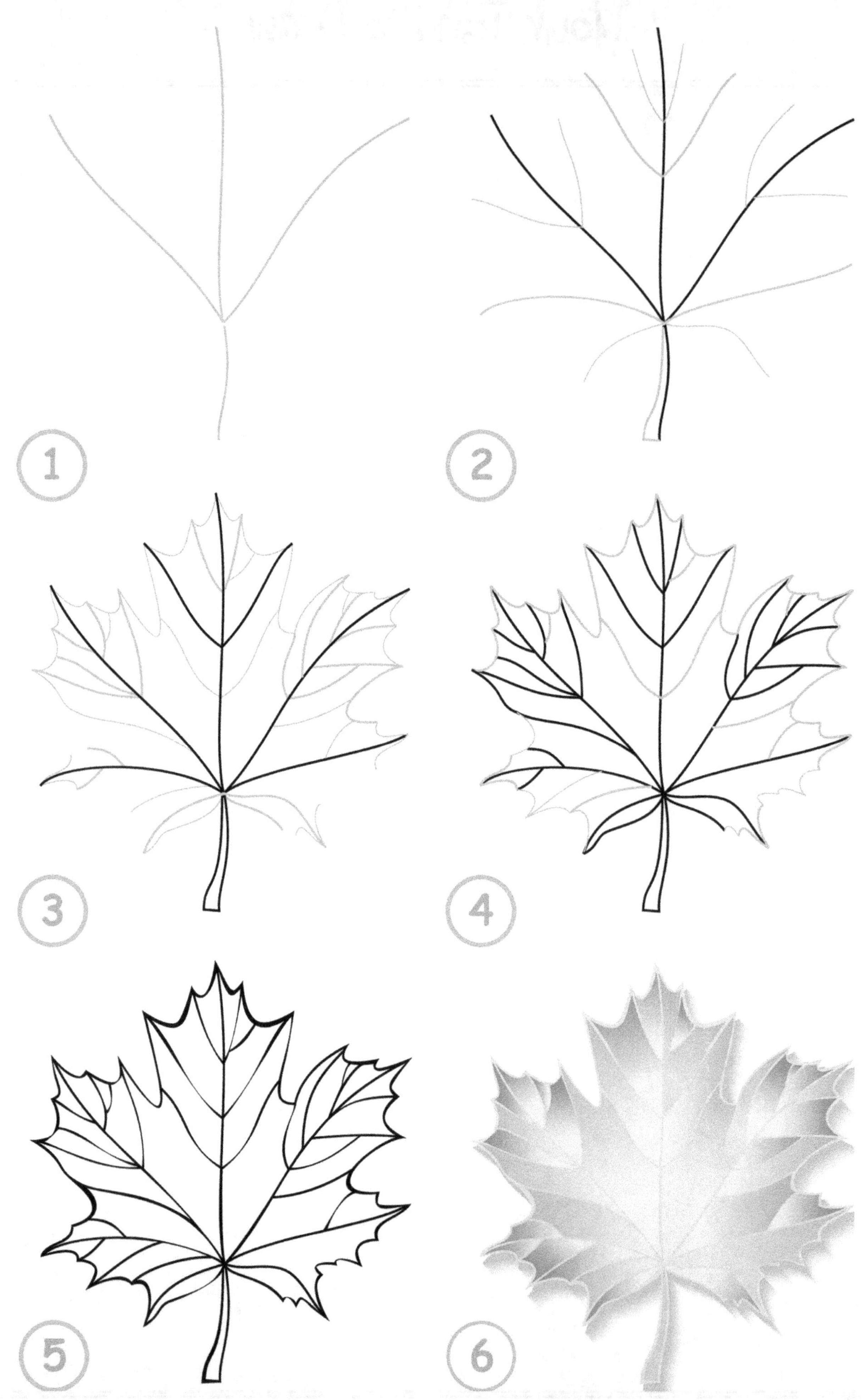

1
2
3
4
5
6

Your Turn to Draw

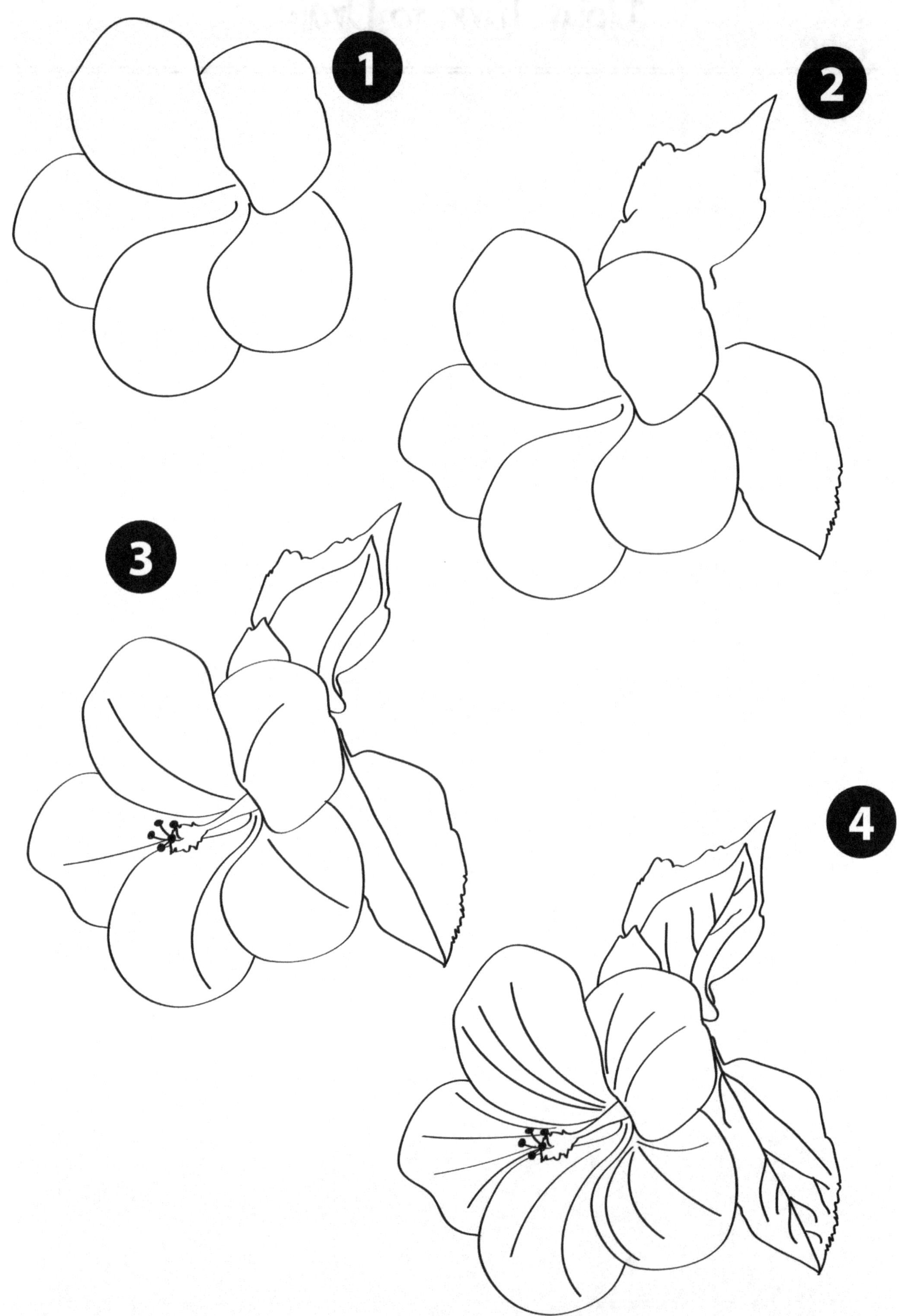

Your Turn to Draw

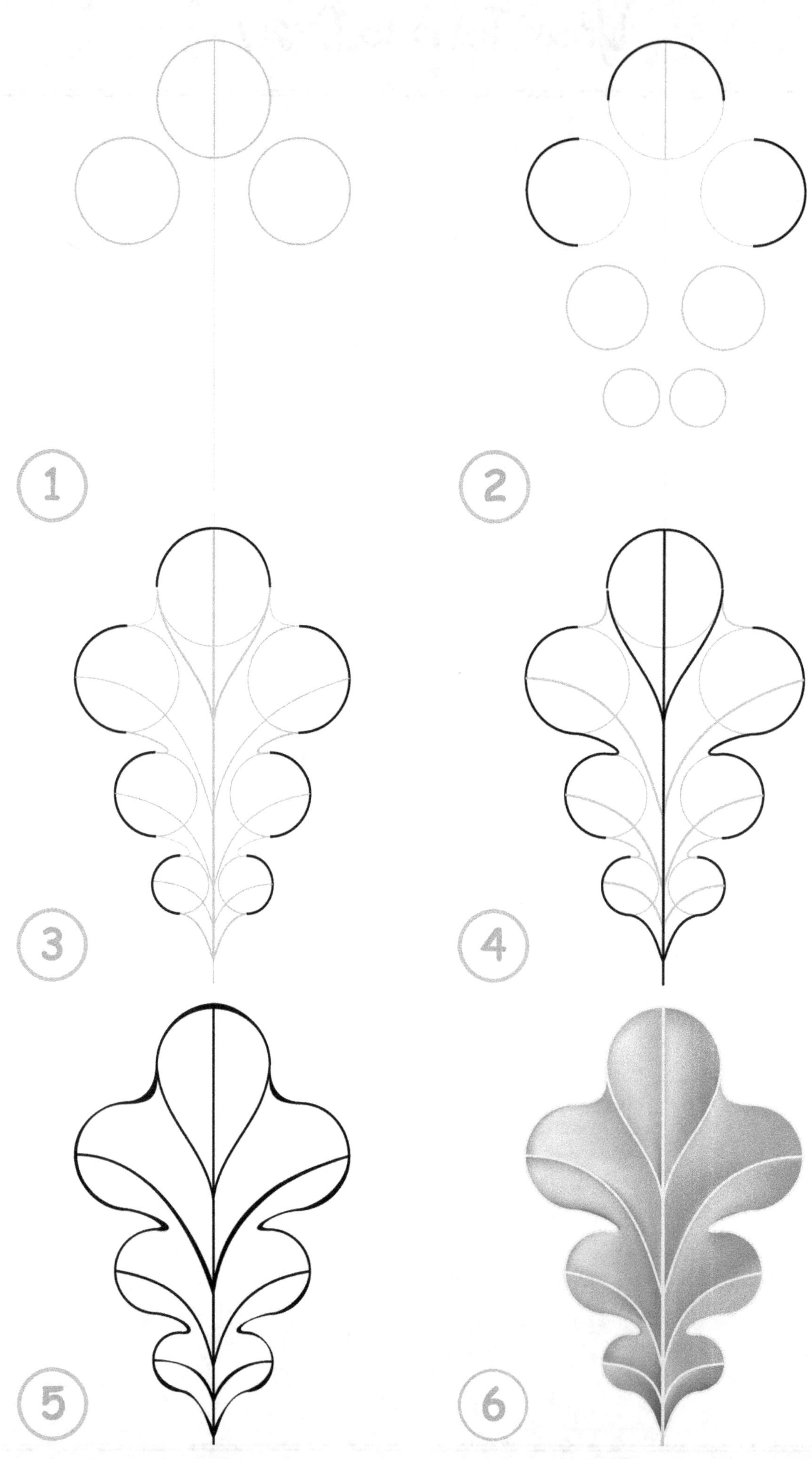

Your Turn to Draw

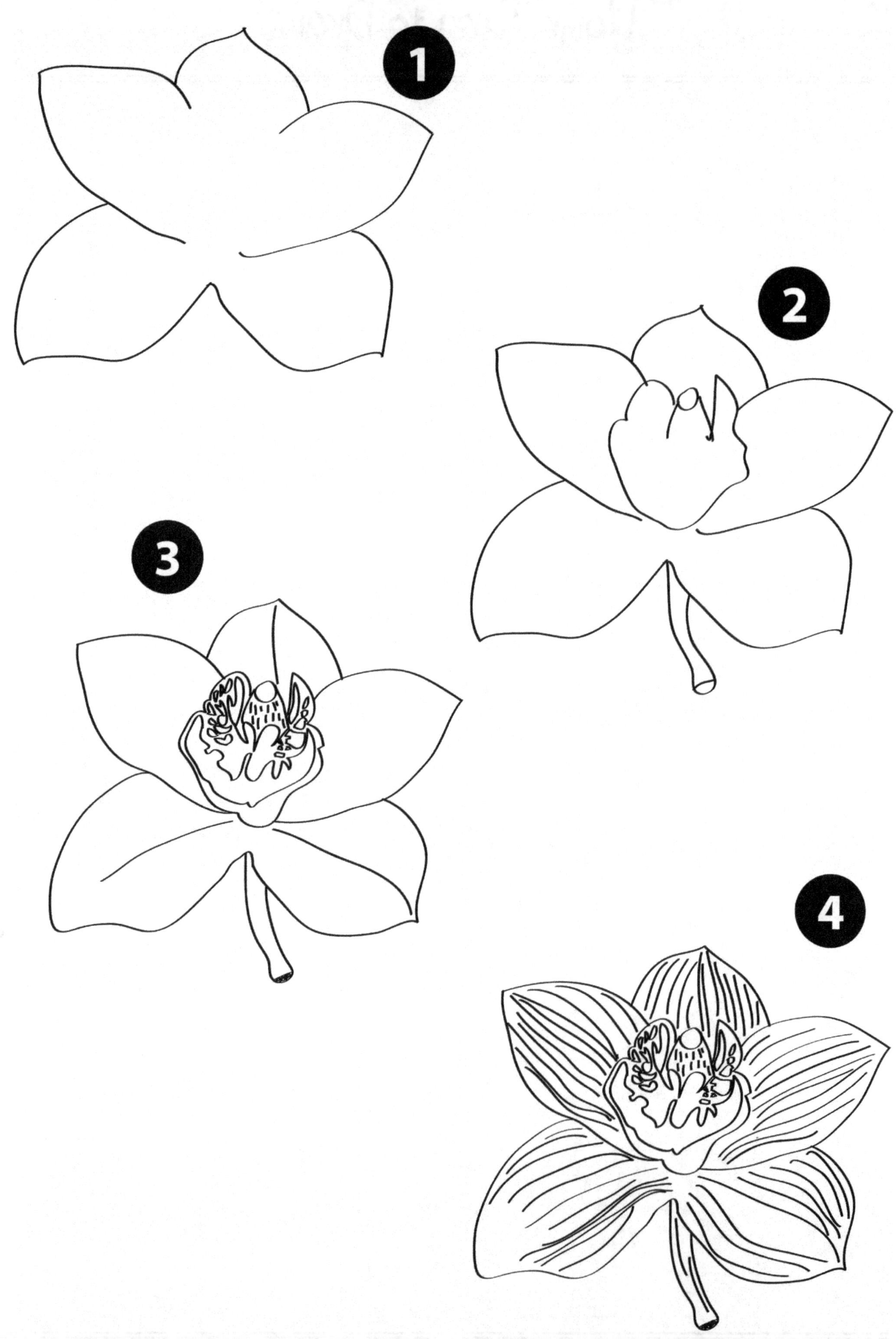
1
2
3
4

Your Turn to Draw

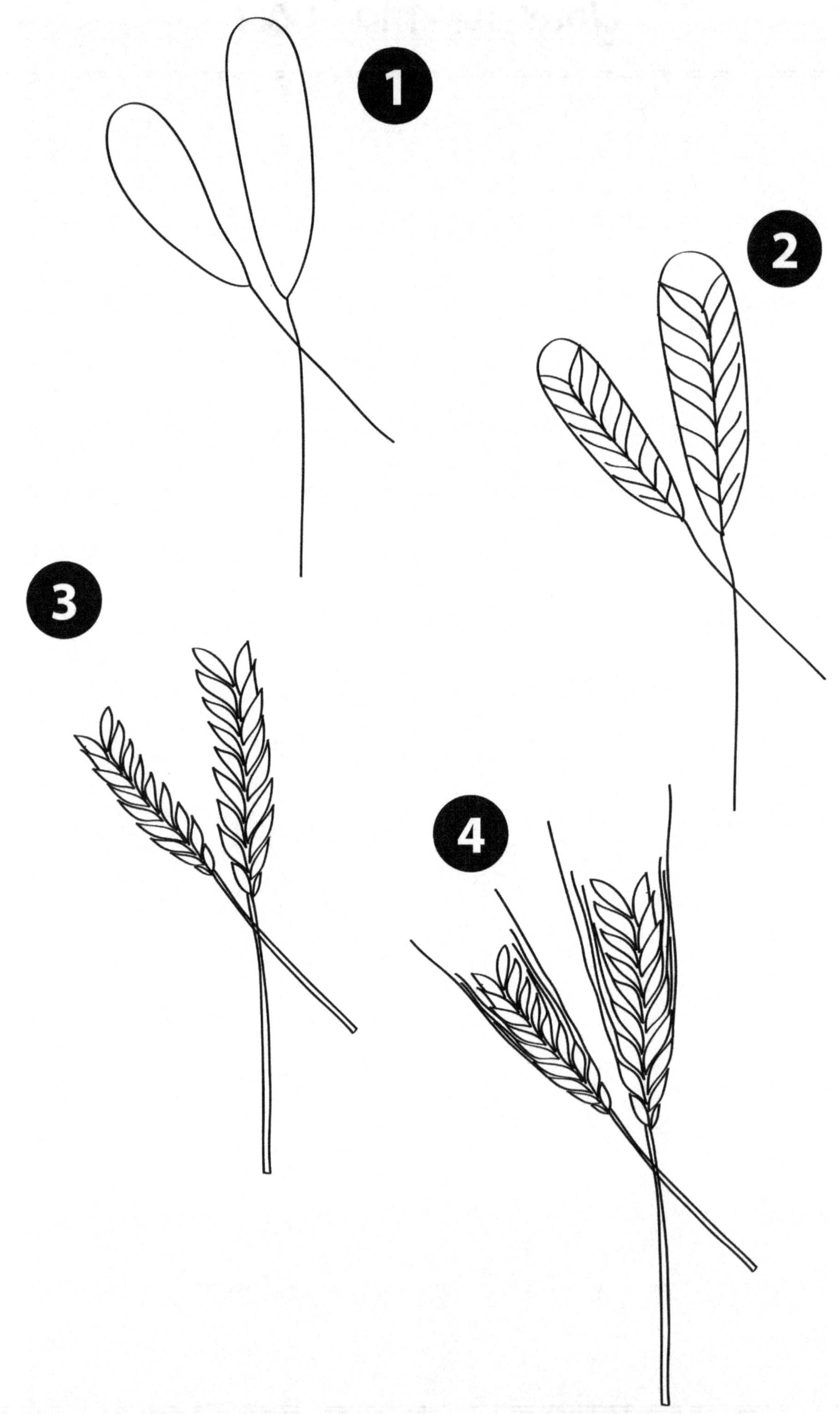

Your Turn to Draw

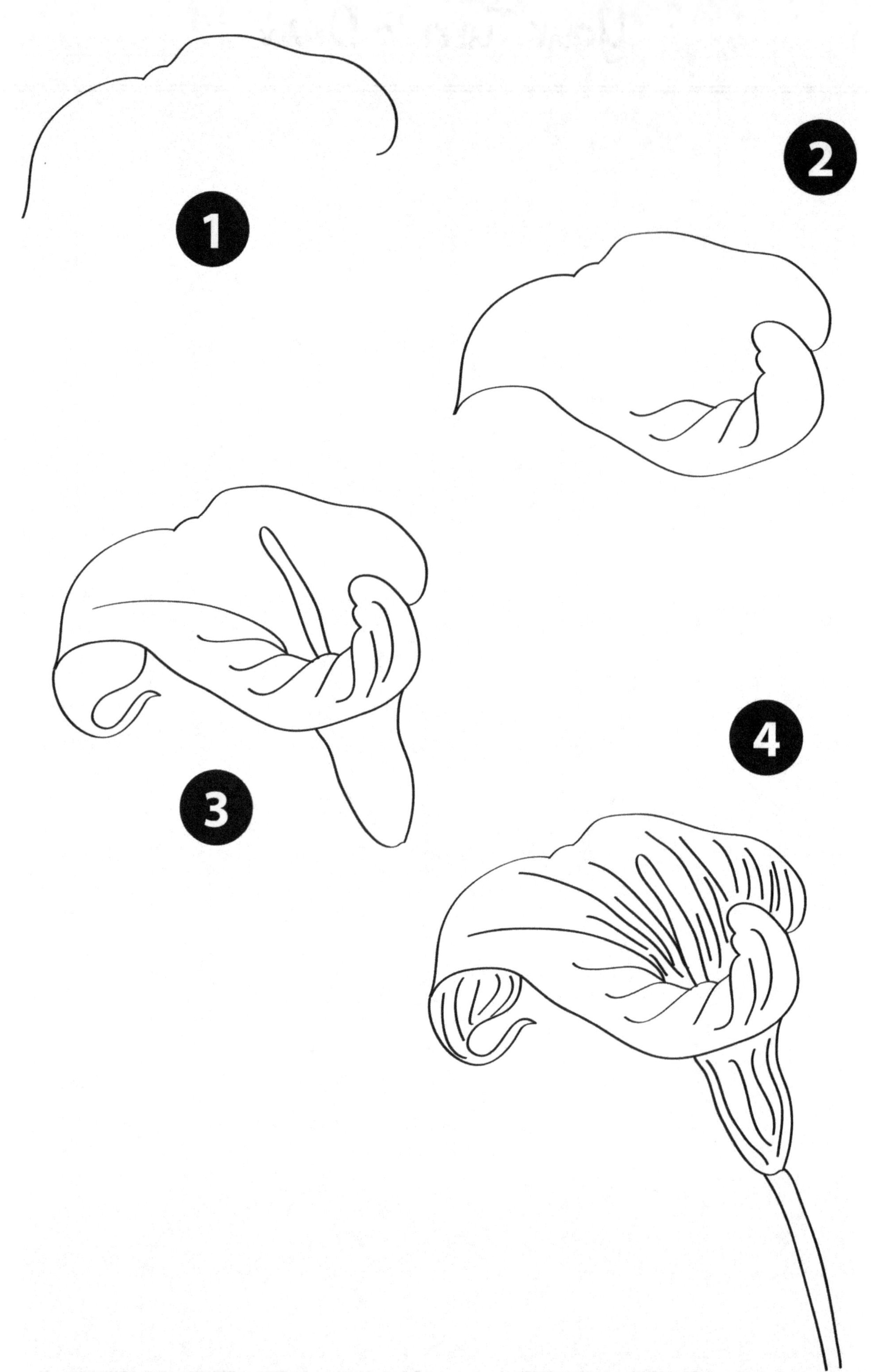

Your Turn to Draw

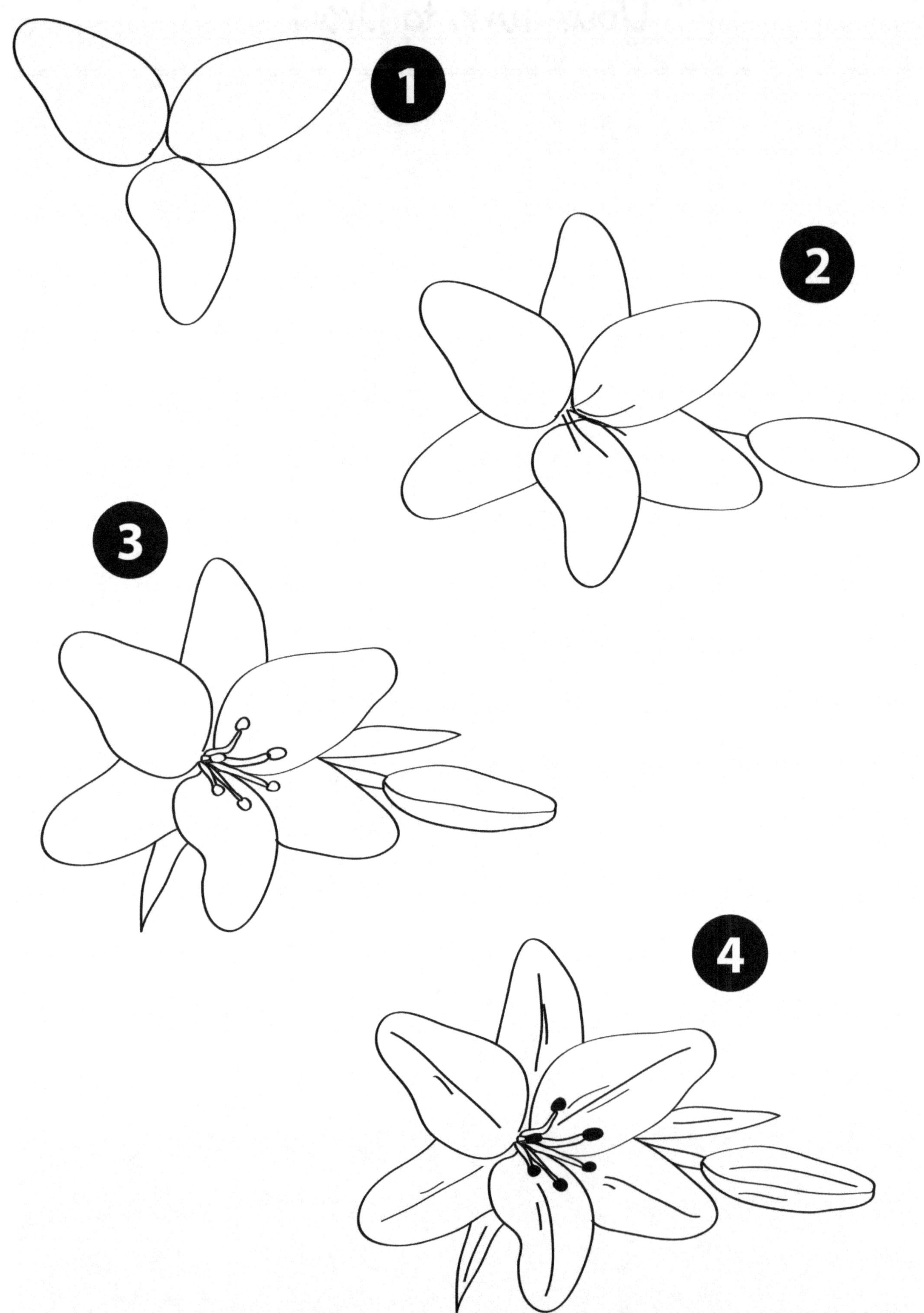

Your Turn to Draw

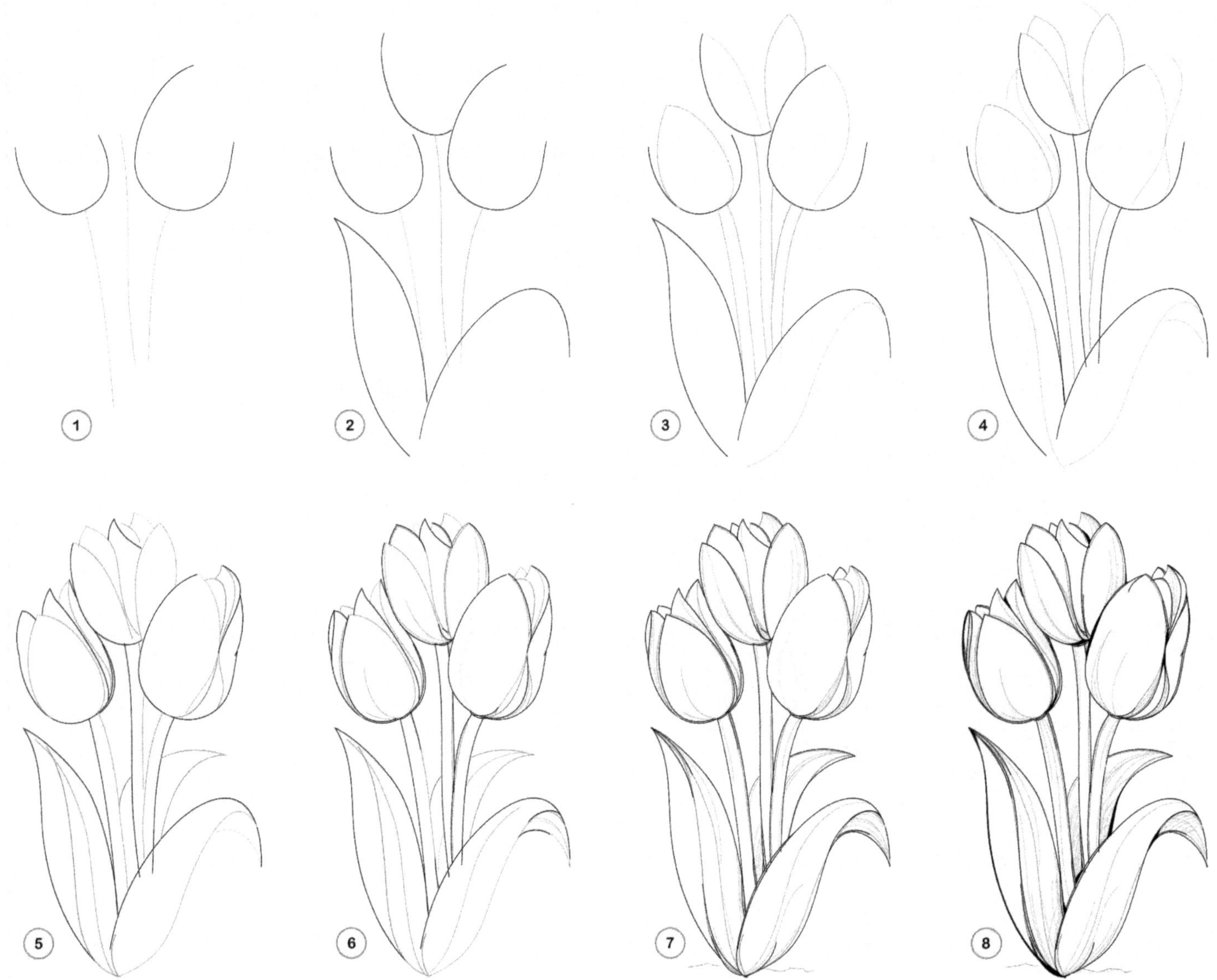

Your Turn to Draw

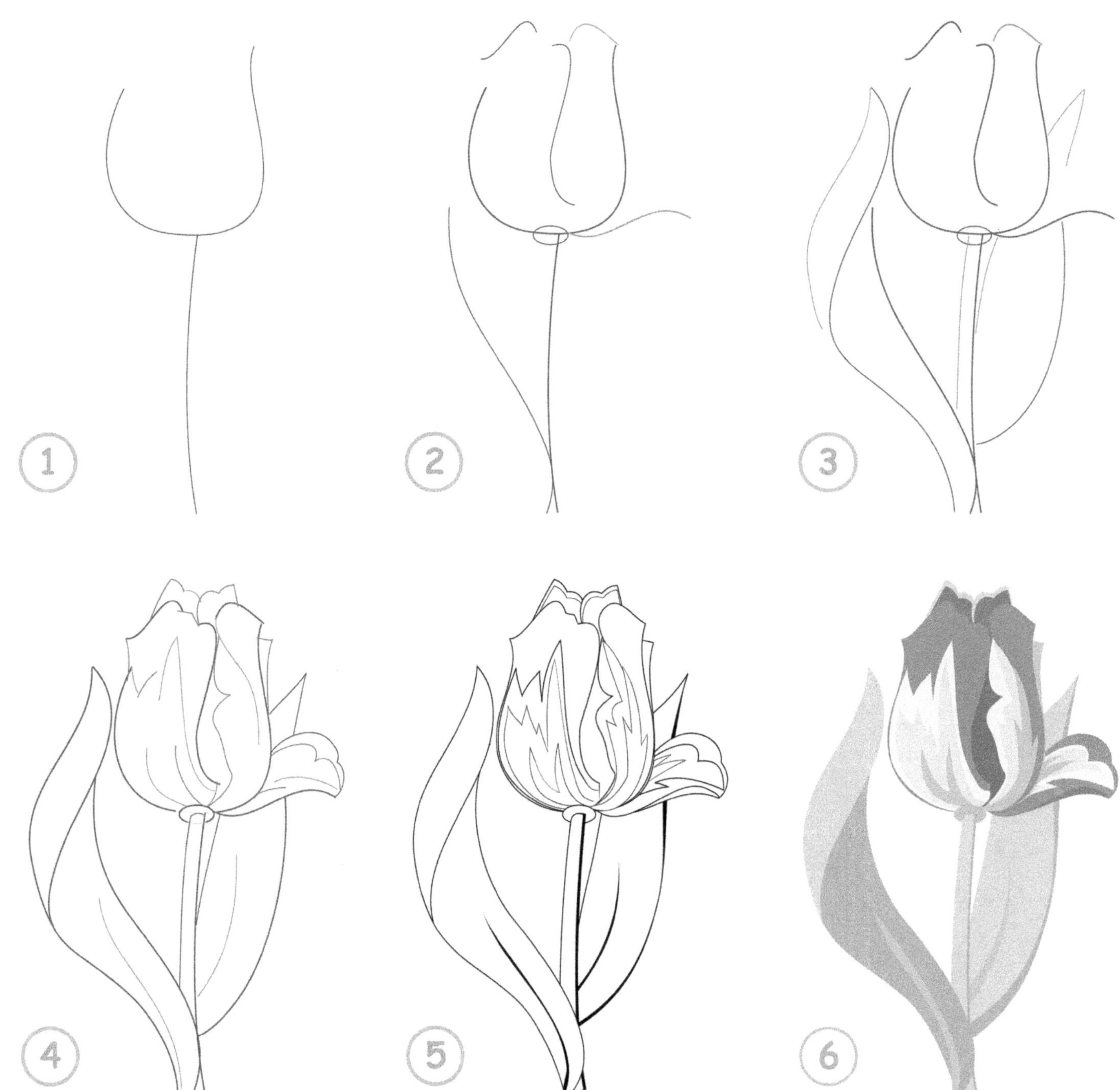

1
2
3
4
5
6

Your Turn to Draw

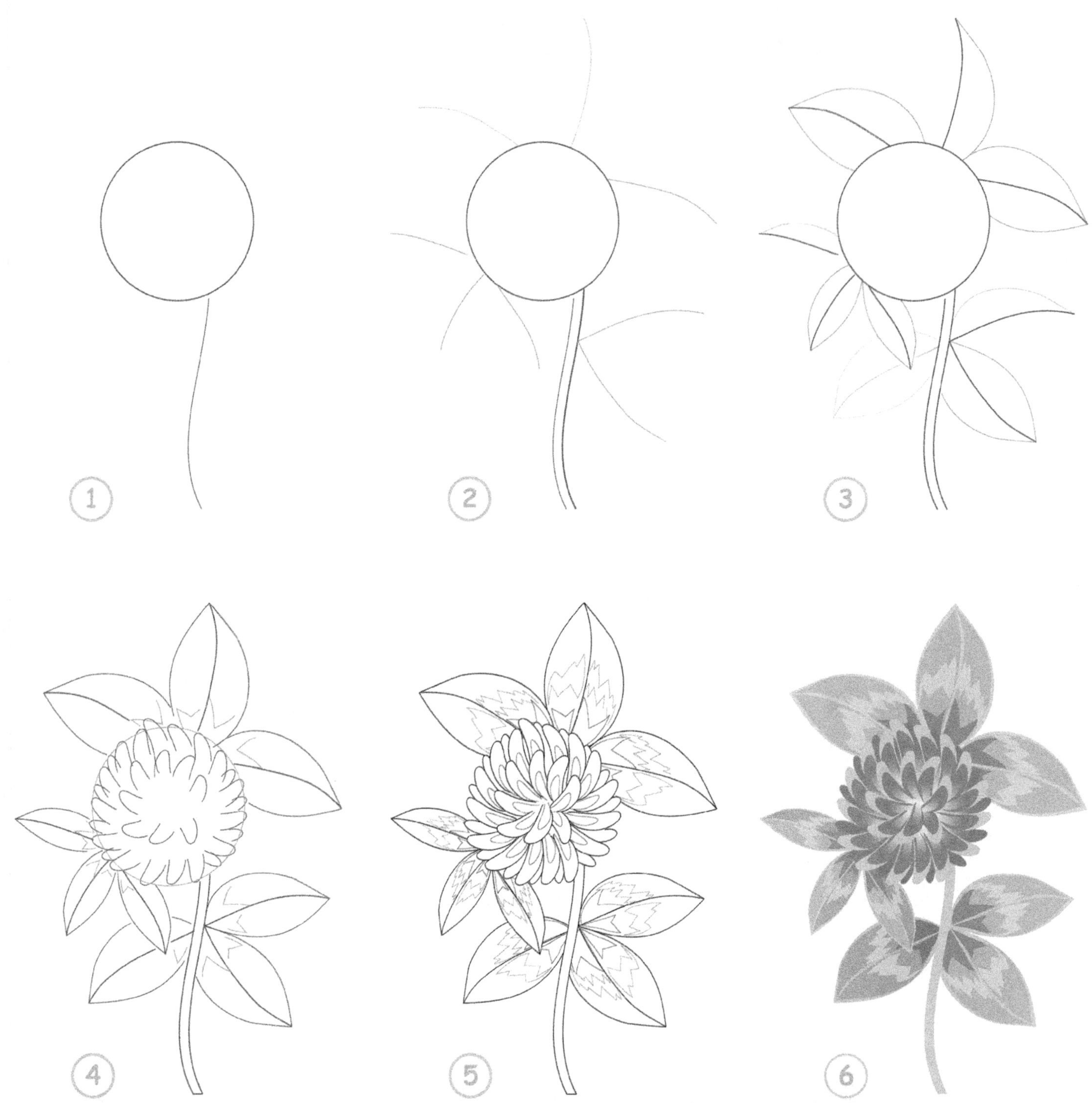

Your Turn to Draw

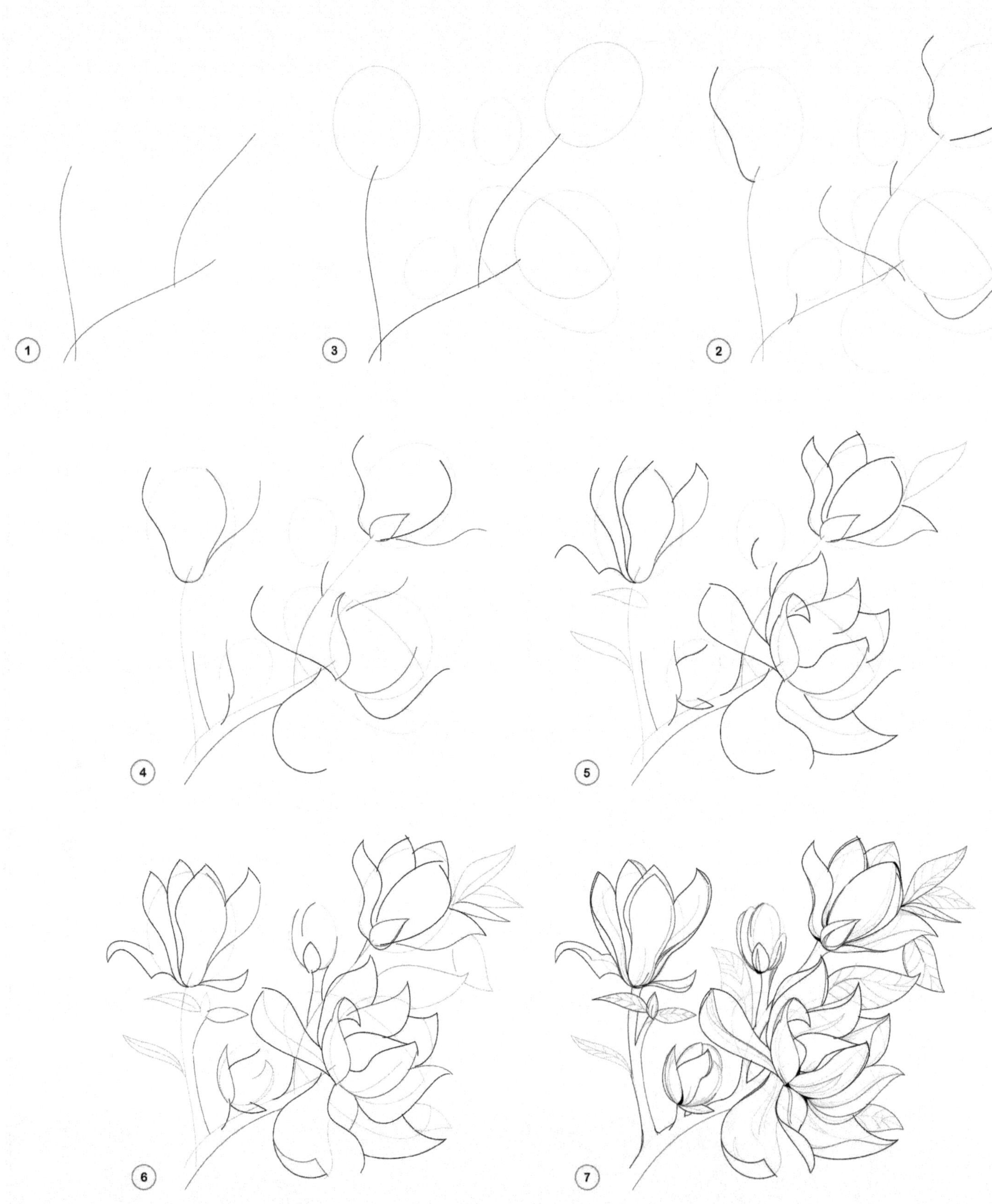

Your Turn to Draw

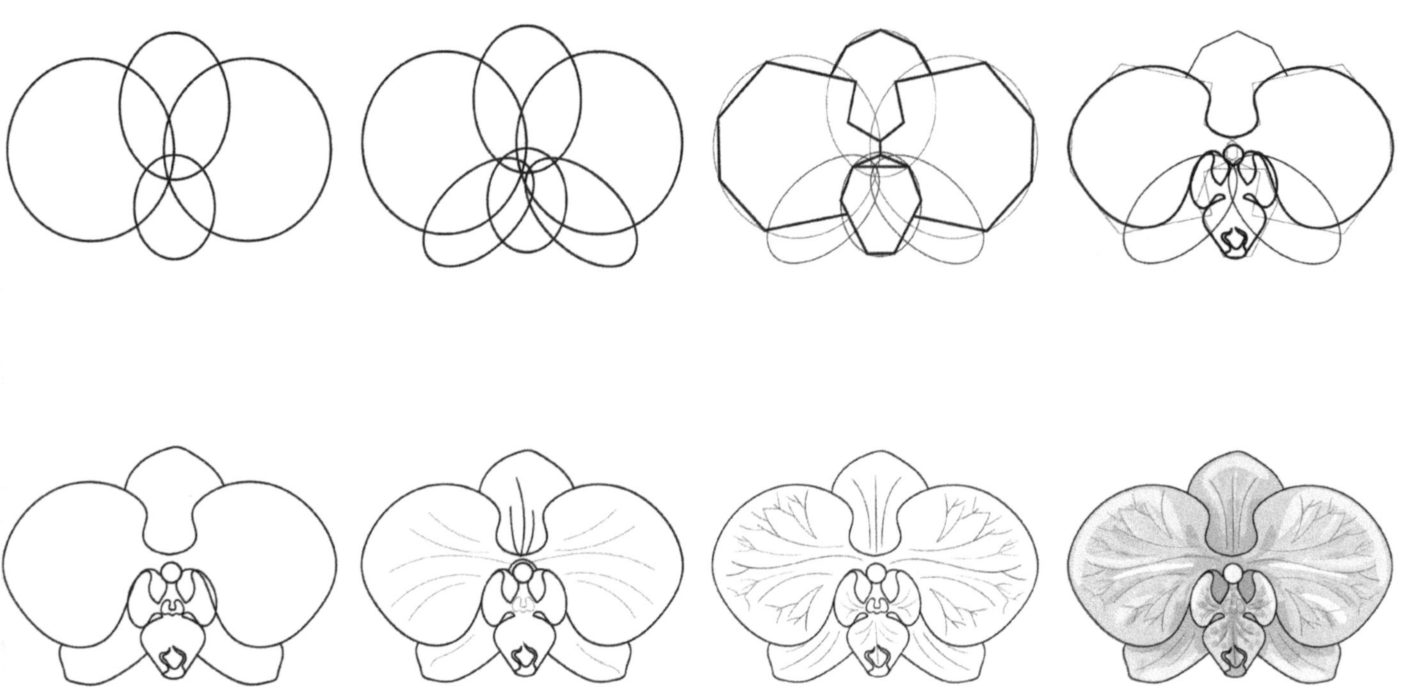

Your Turn to Draw

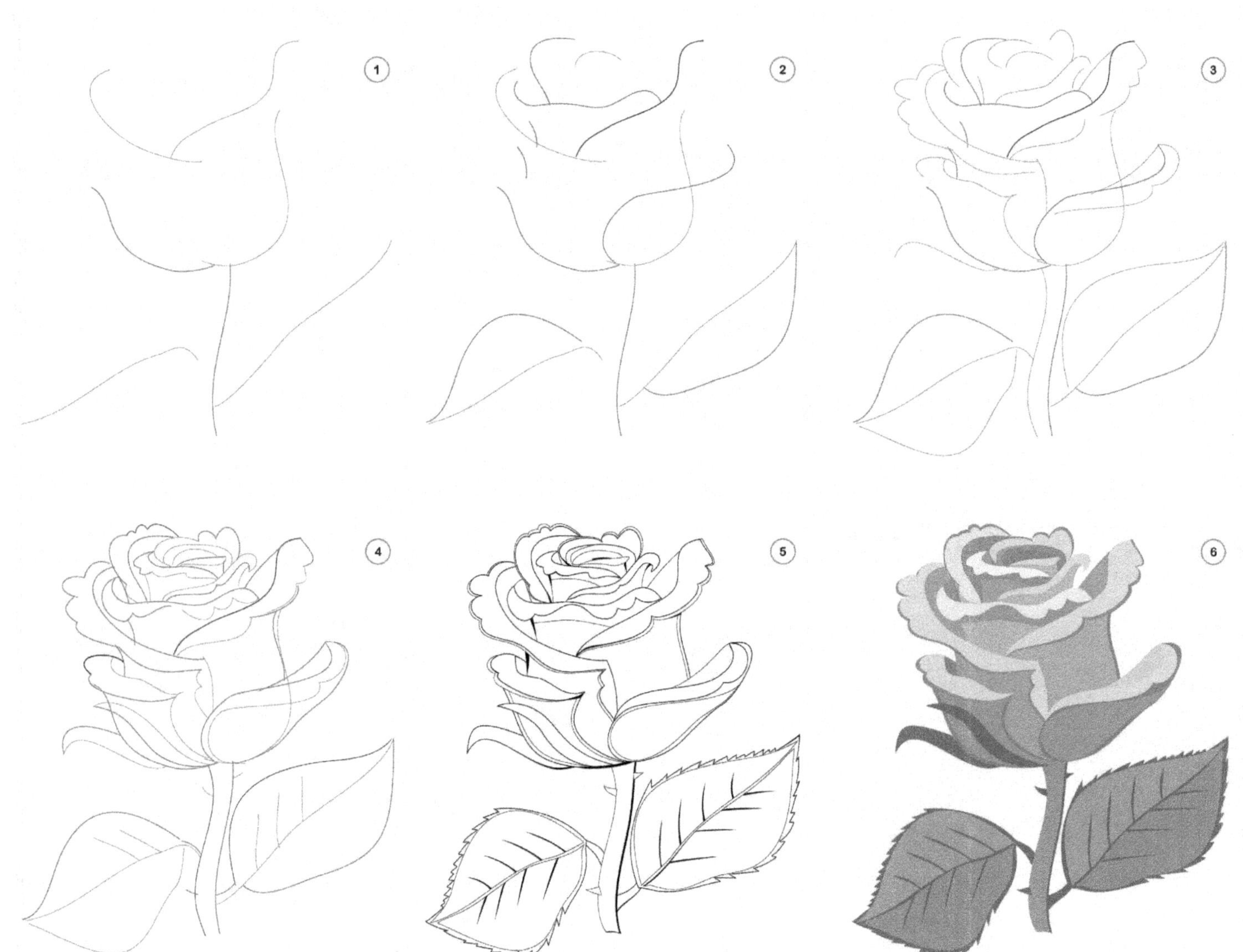

Your Turn to Draw

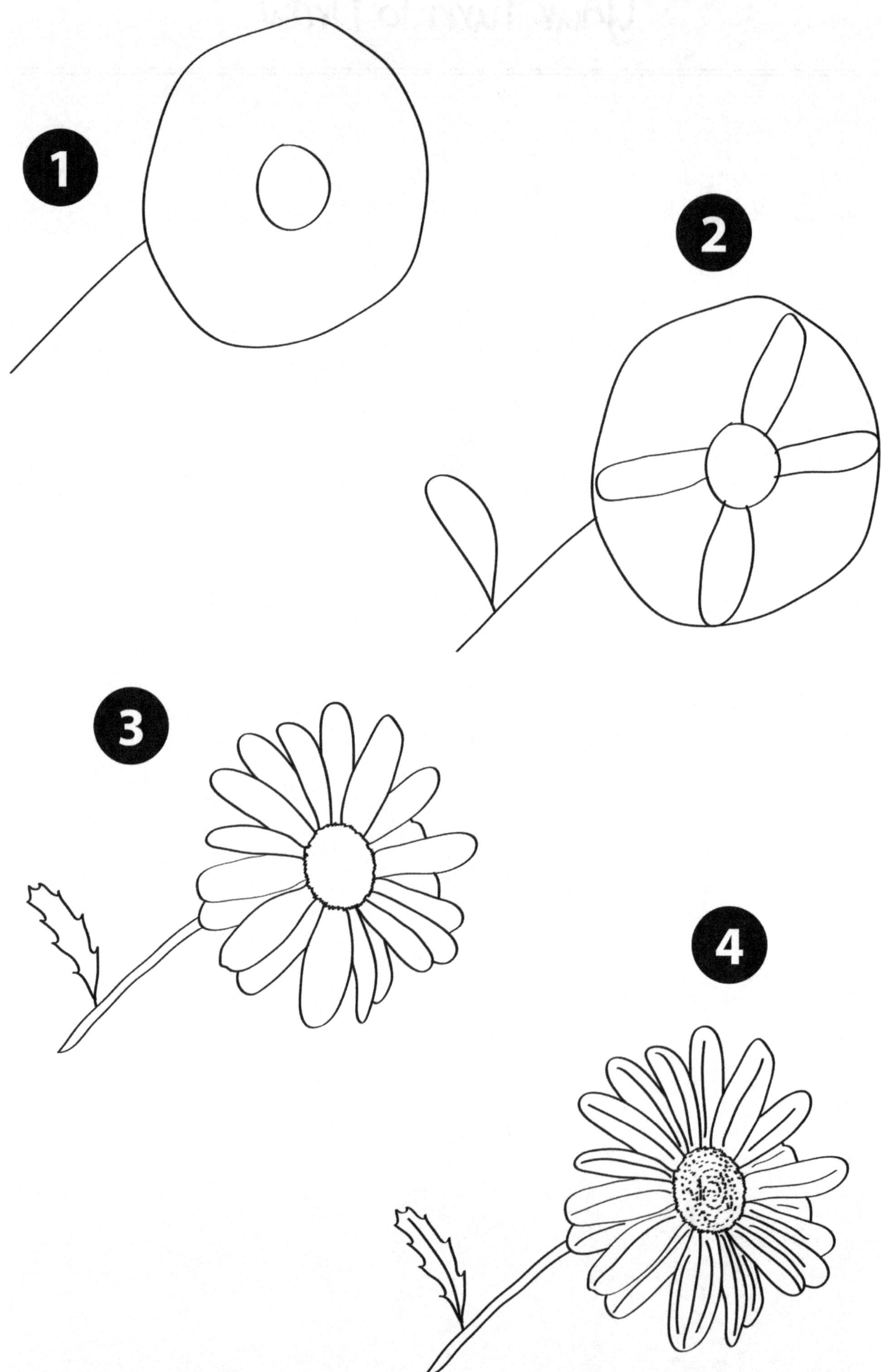
1
2
3
4

Your Turn to Draw

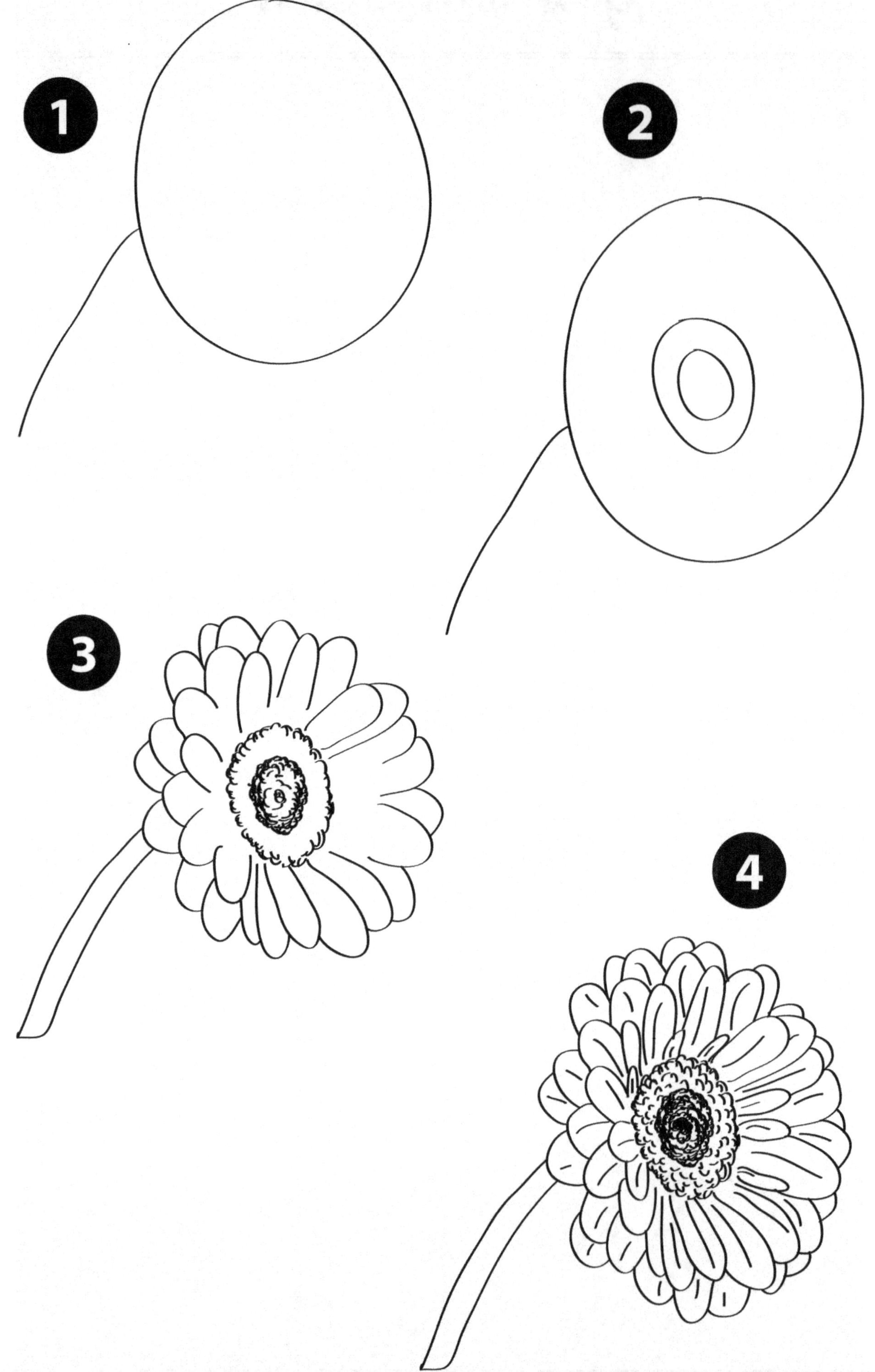

Your Turn to Draw

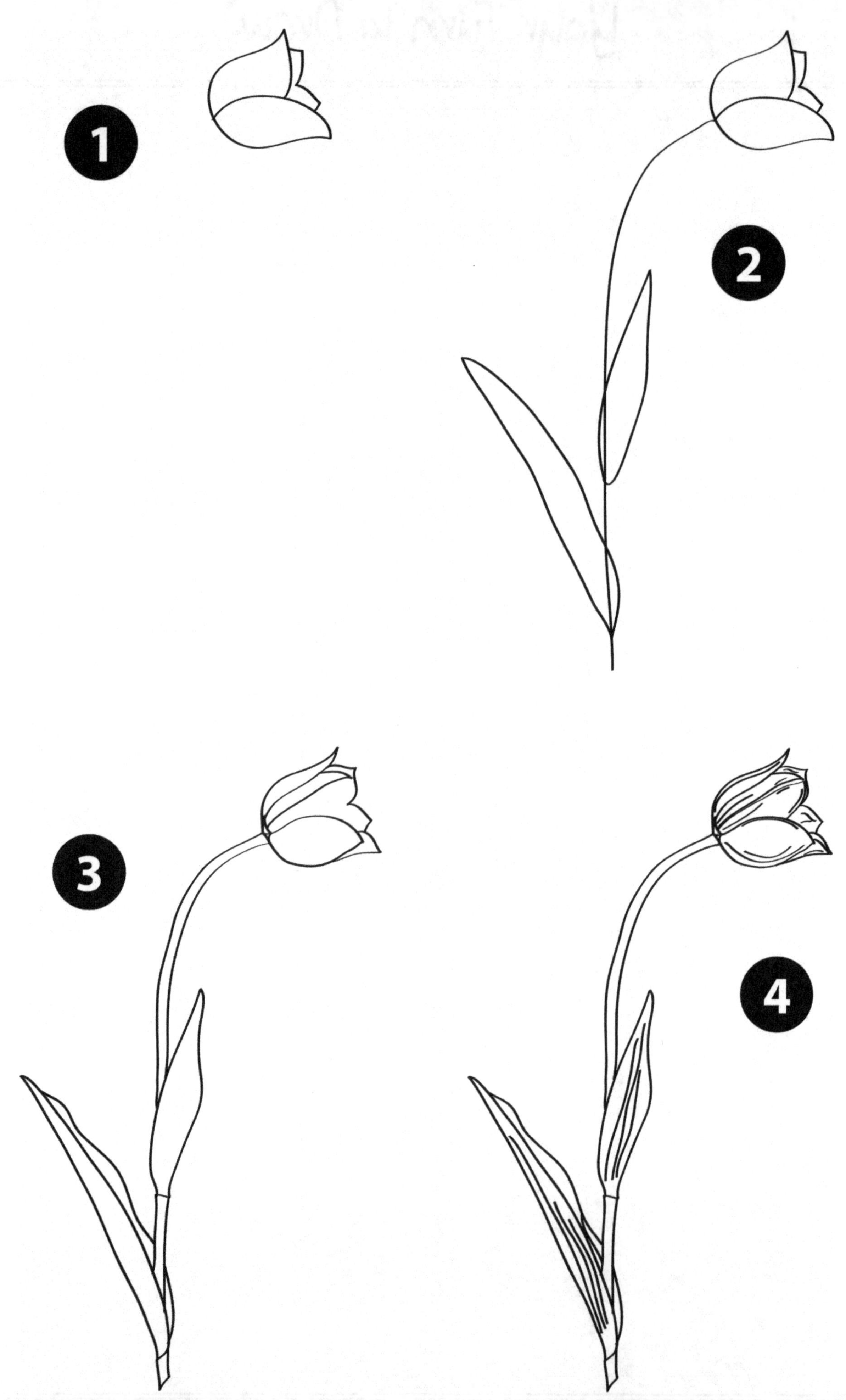

Your Turn to Draw

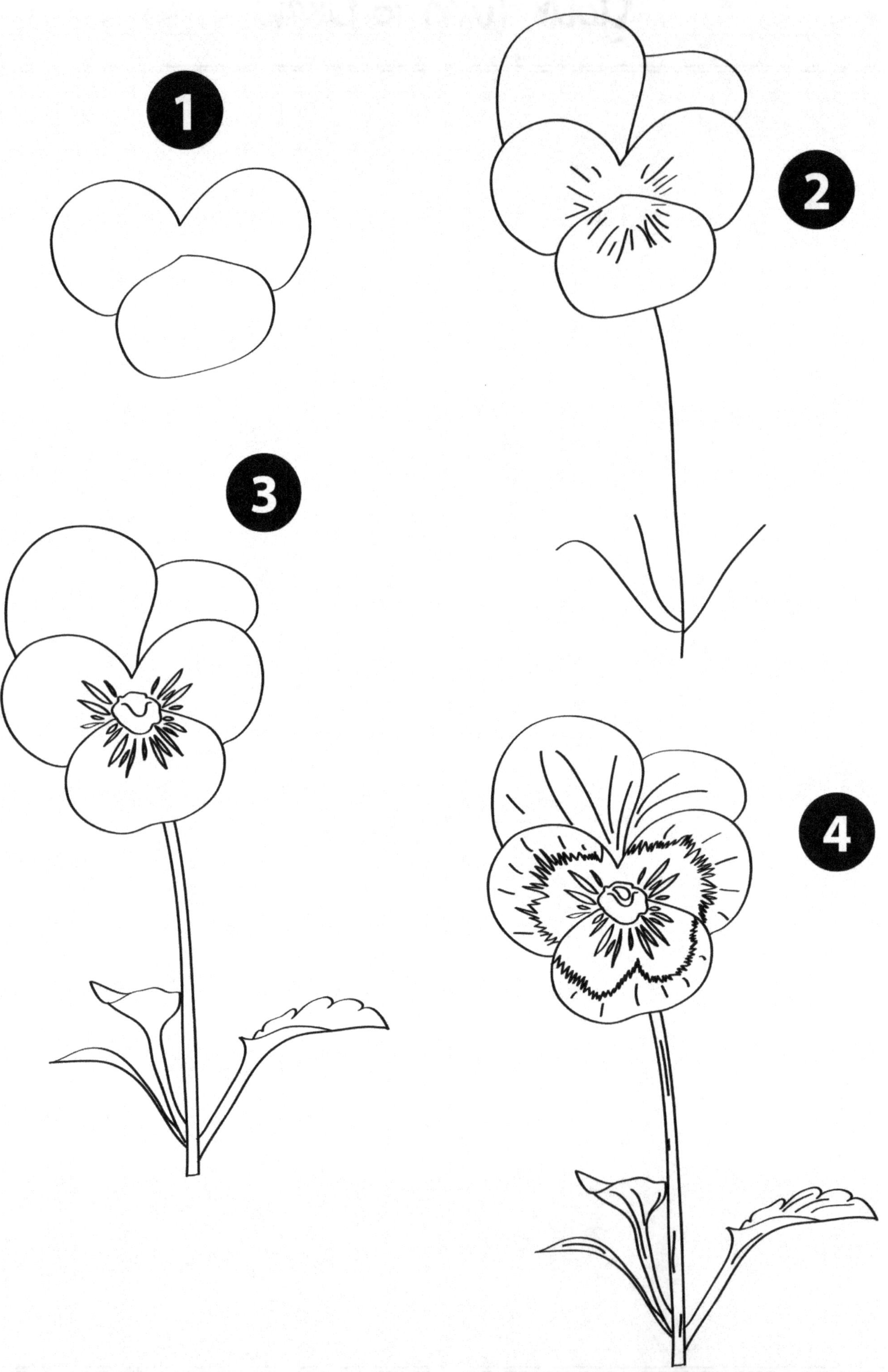

Your Turn to Draw

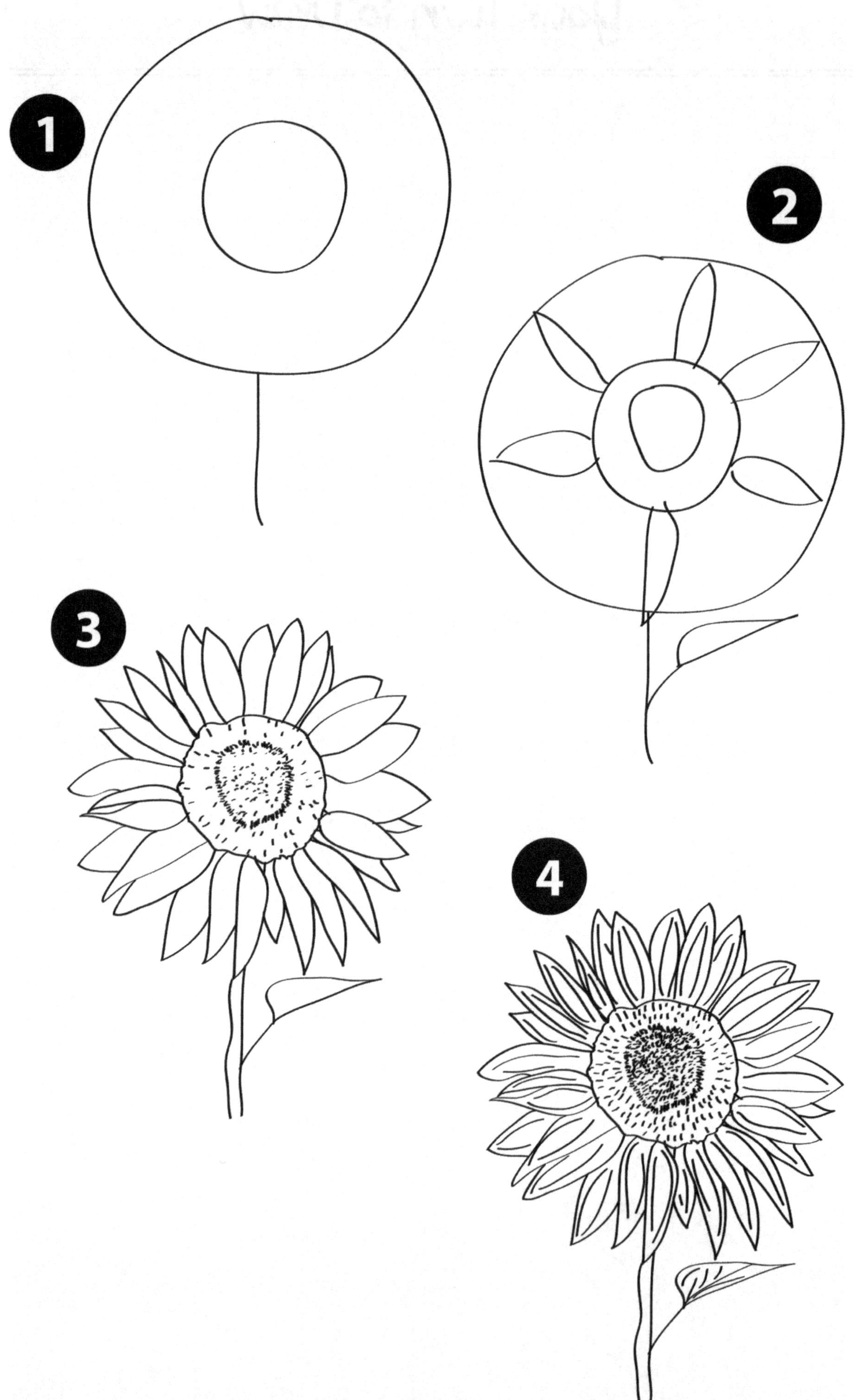

1
2
3
4

Your Turn to Draw

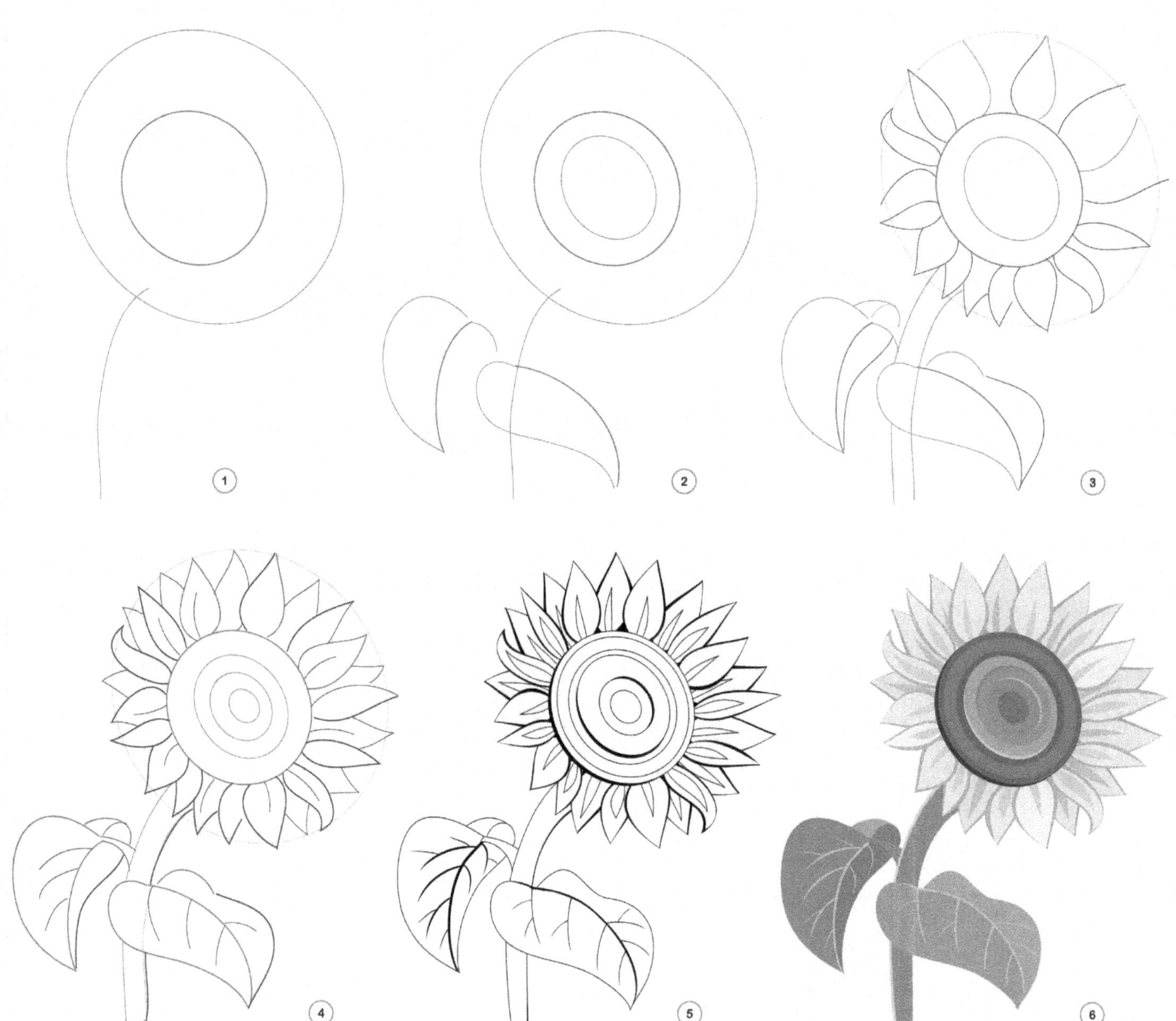

Your Turn to Draw

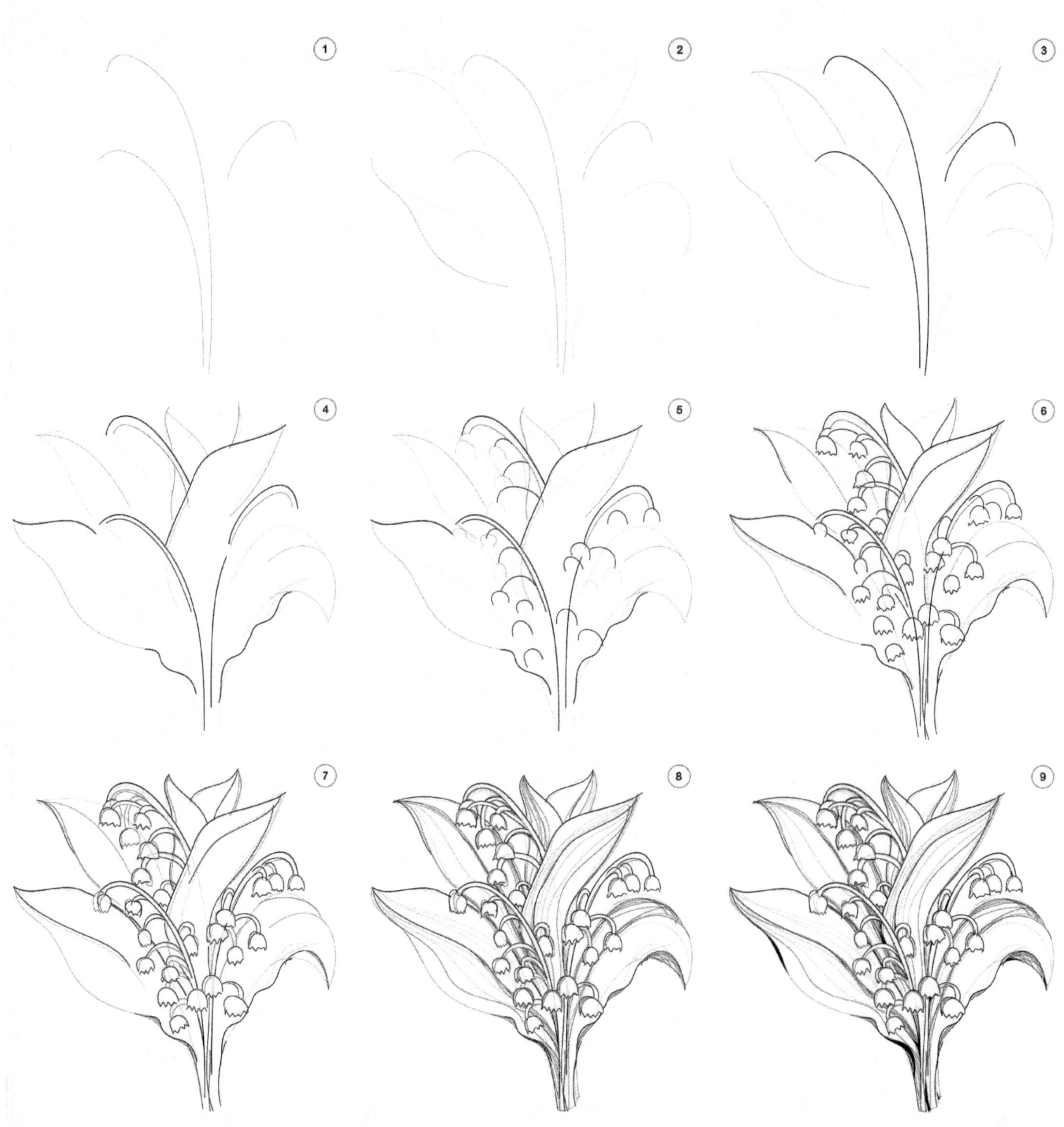

Your Turn to Draw

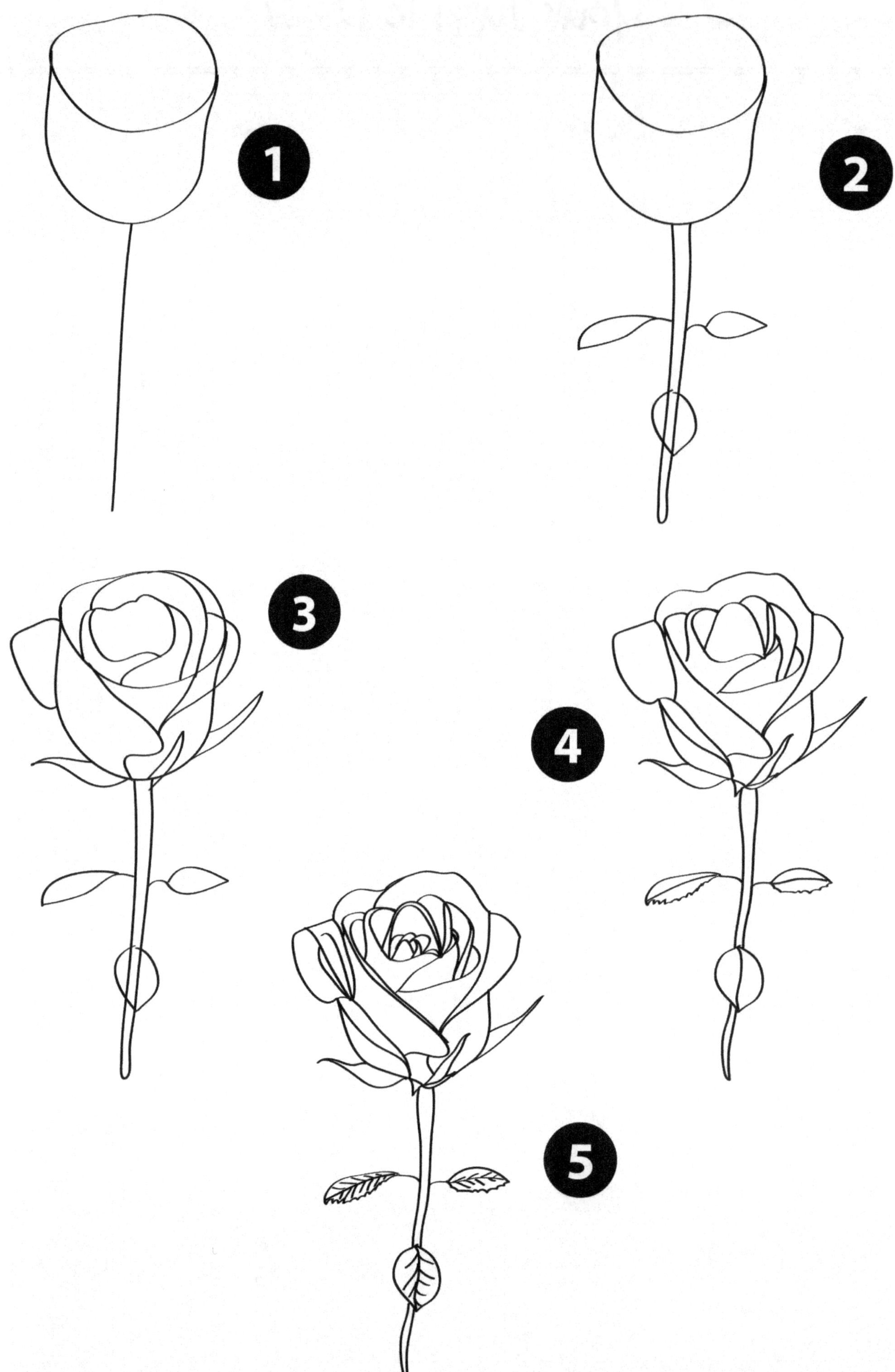

Your Turn to Draw

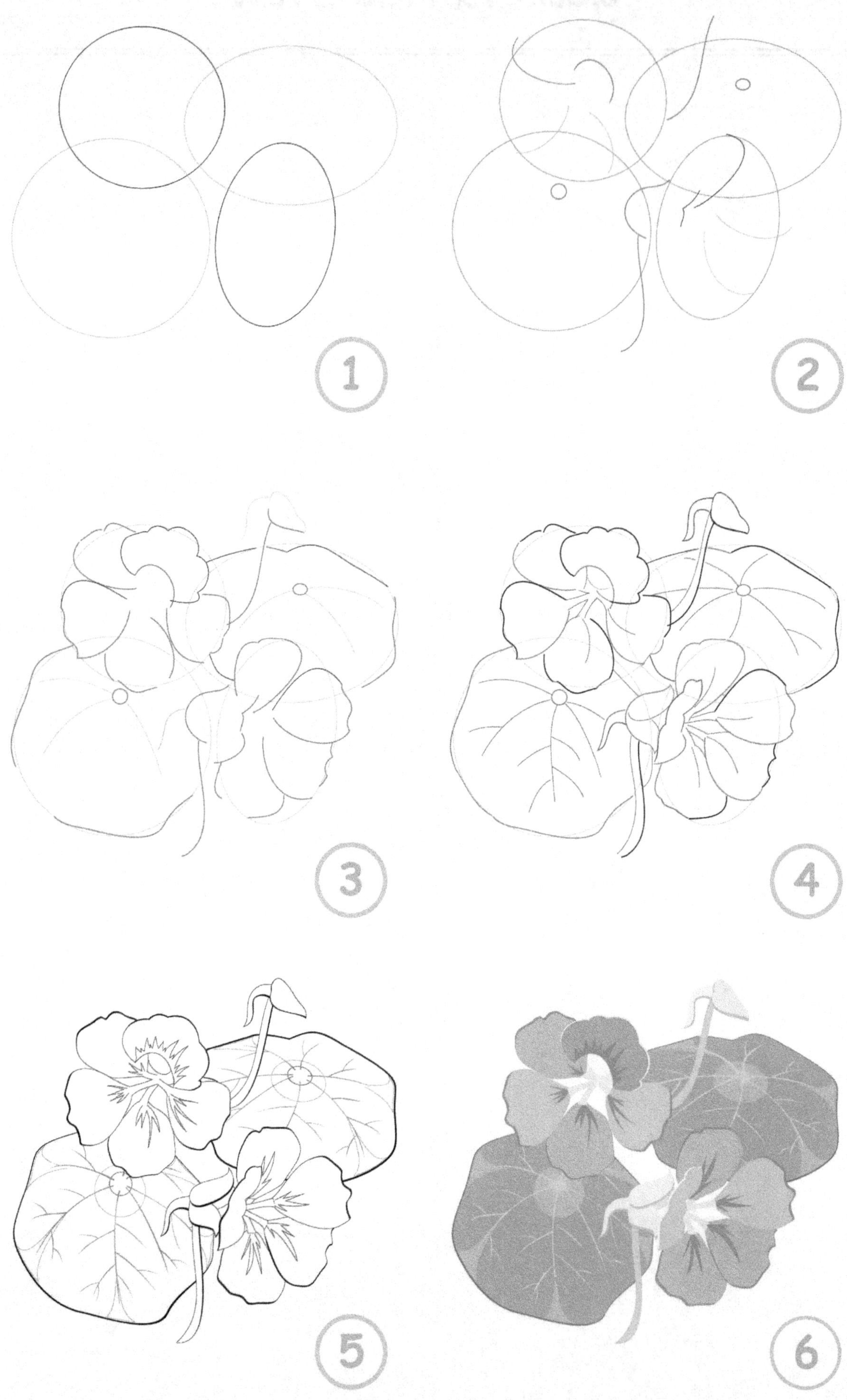

Your Turn to Draw

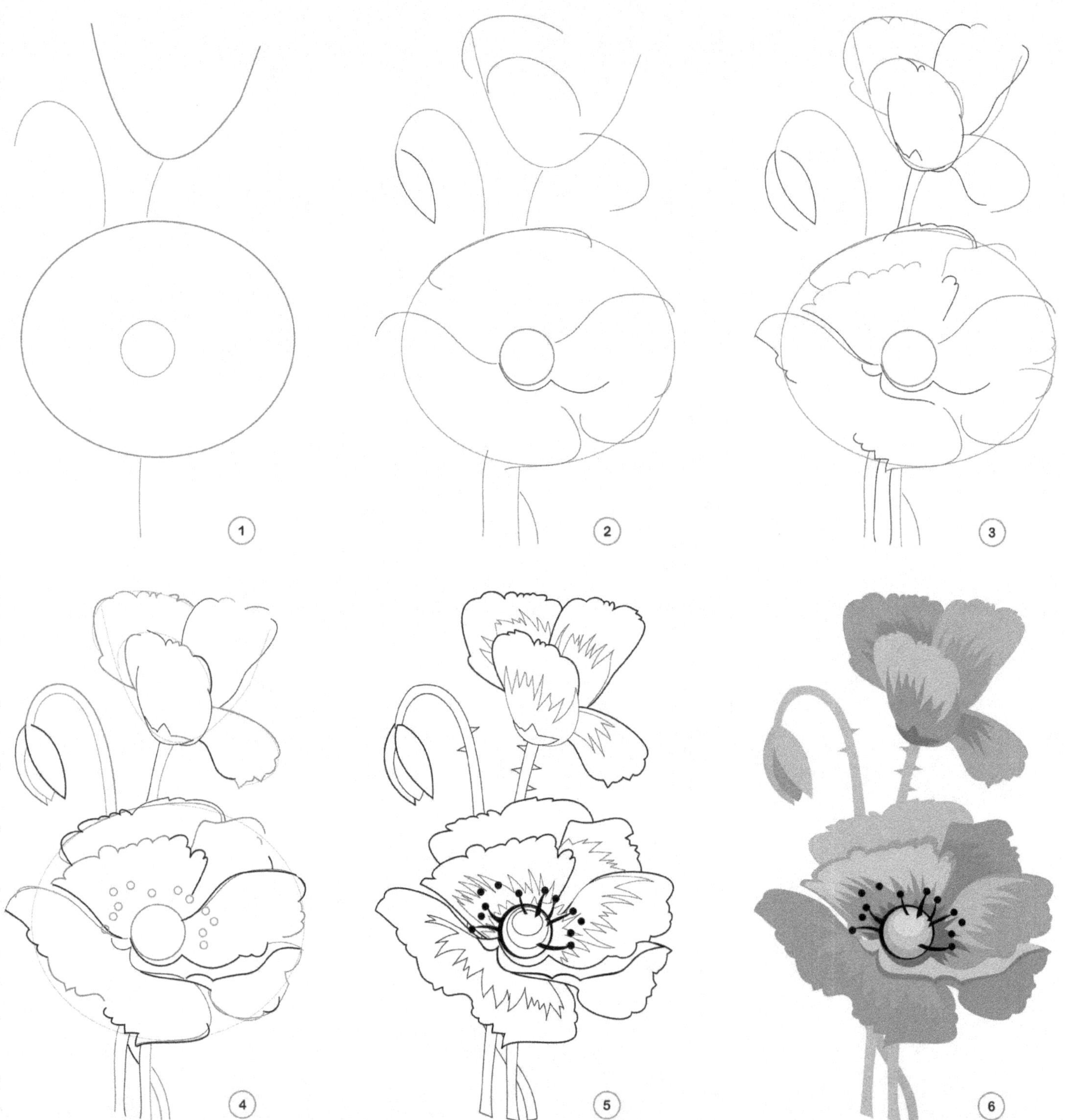

Your Turn to Draw

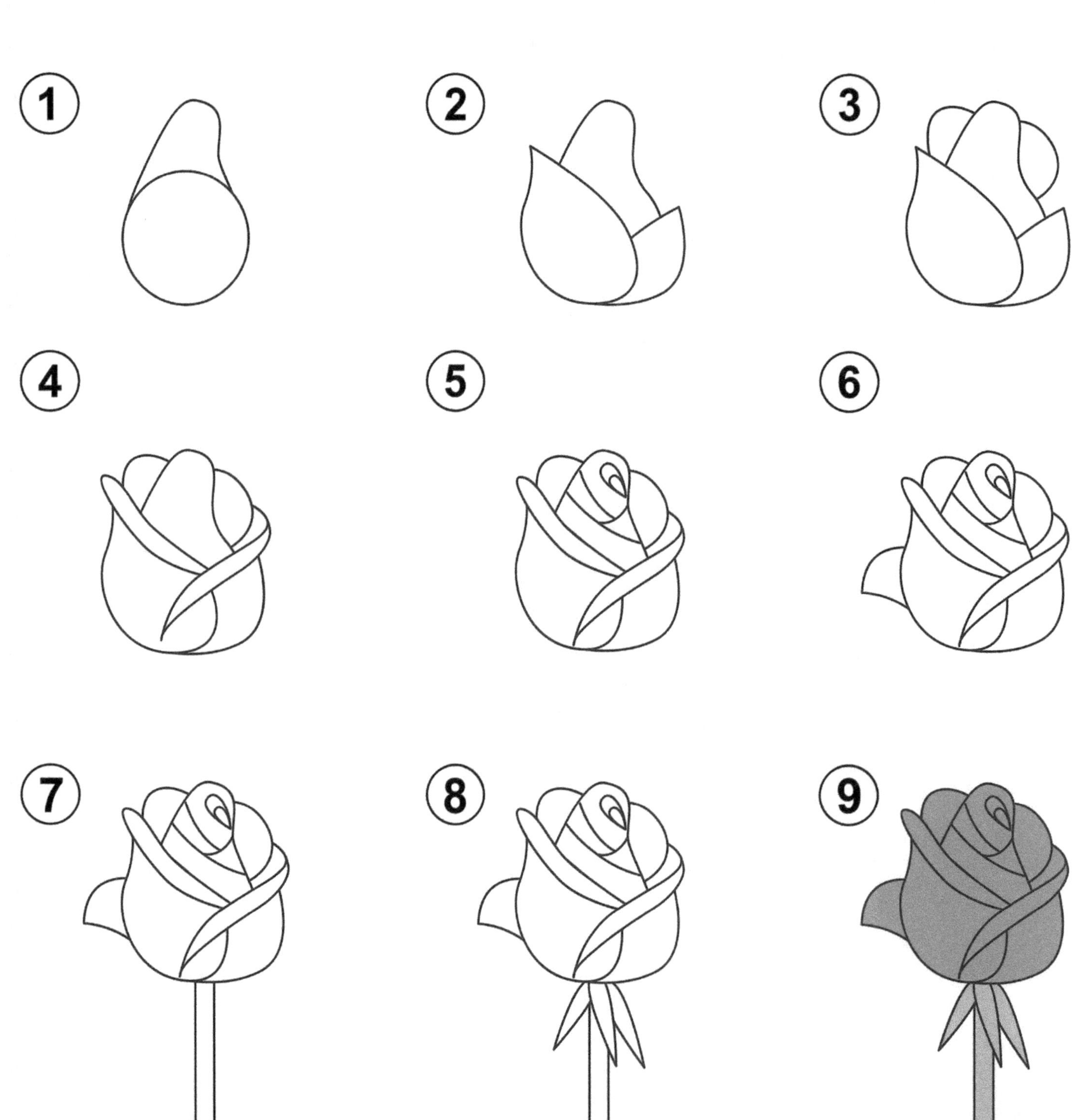

Your Turn to Draw

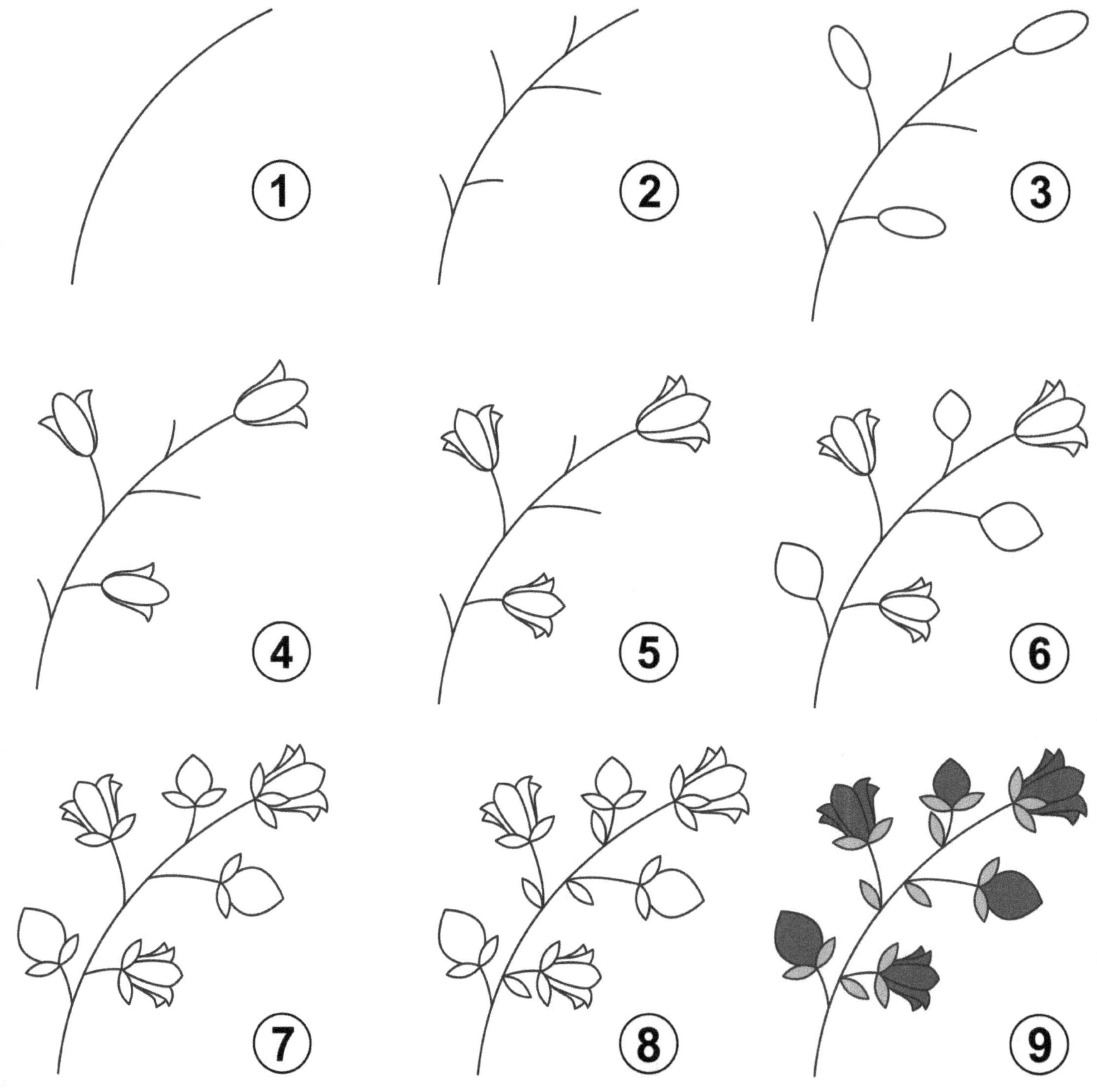

Your Turn to Draw

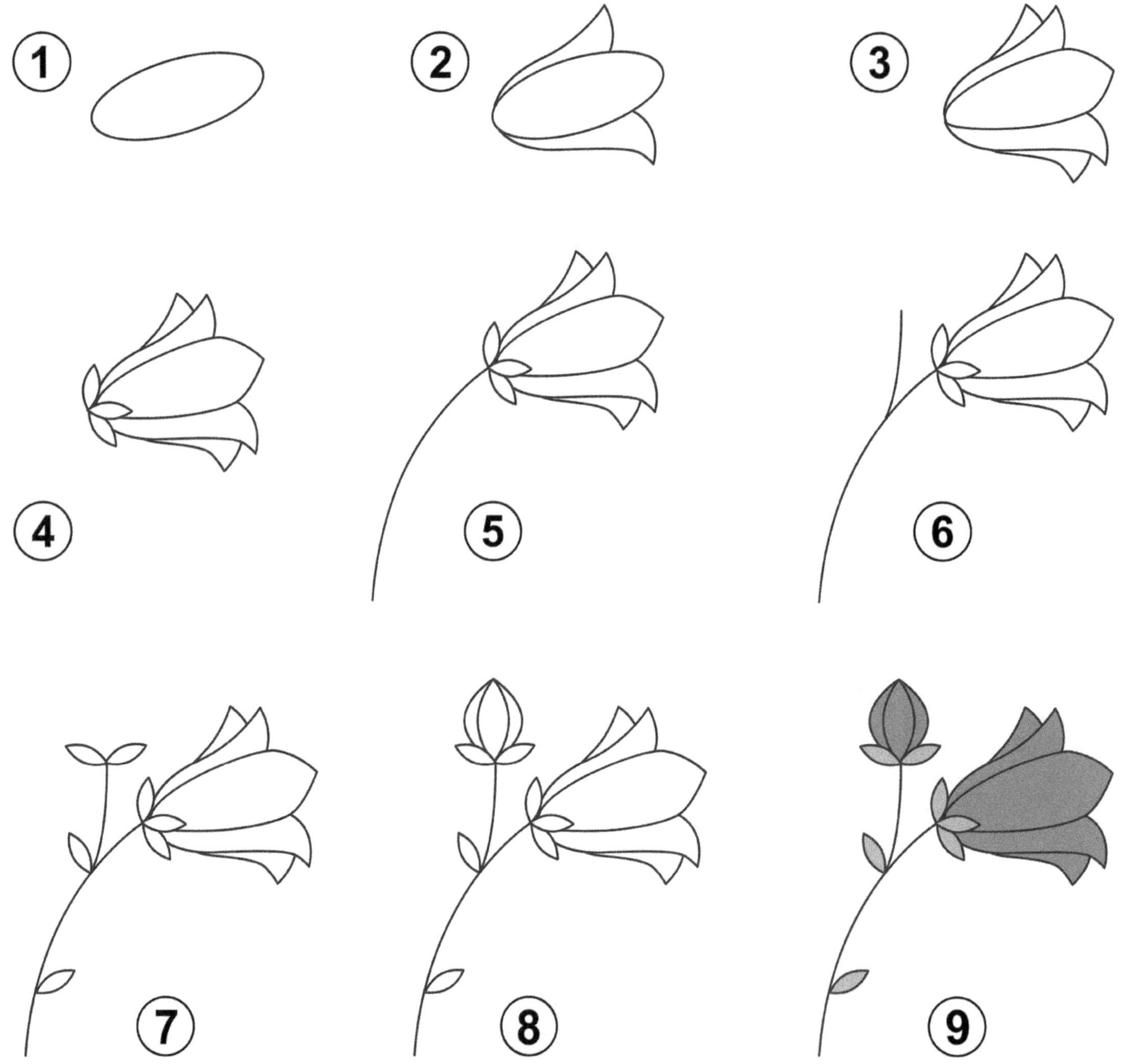

Your Turn to Draw

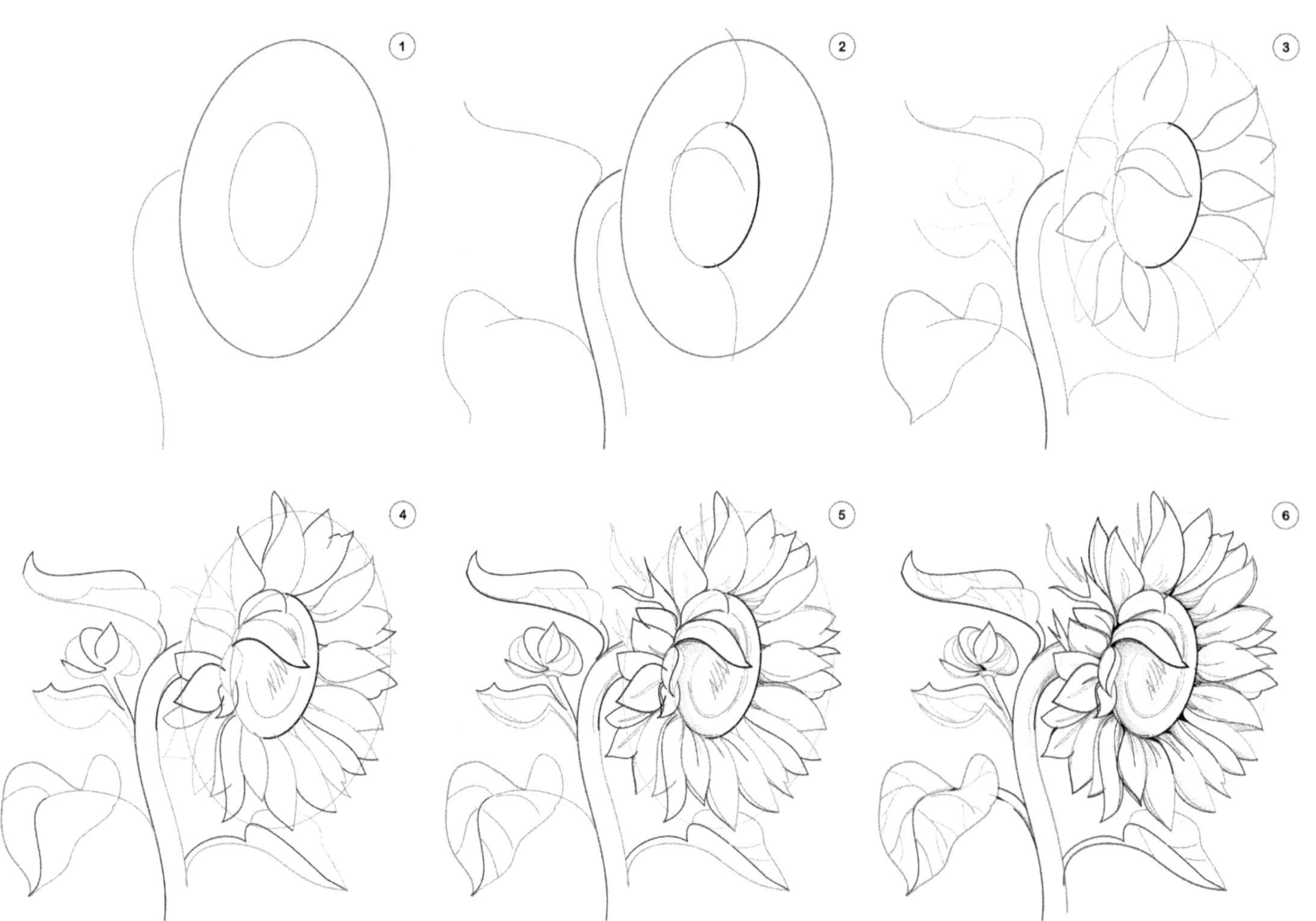

Your Turn to Draw

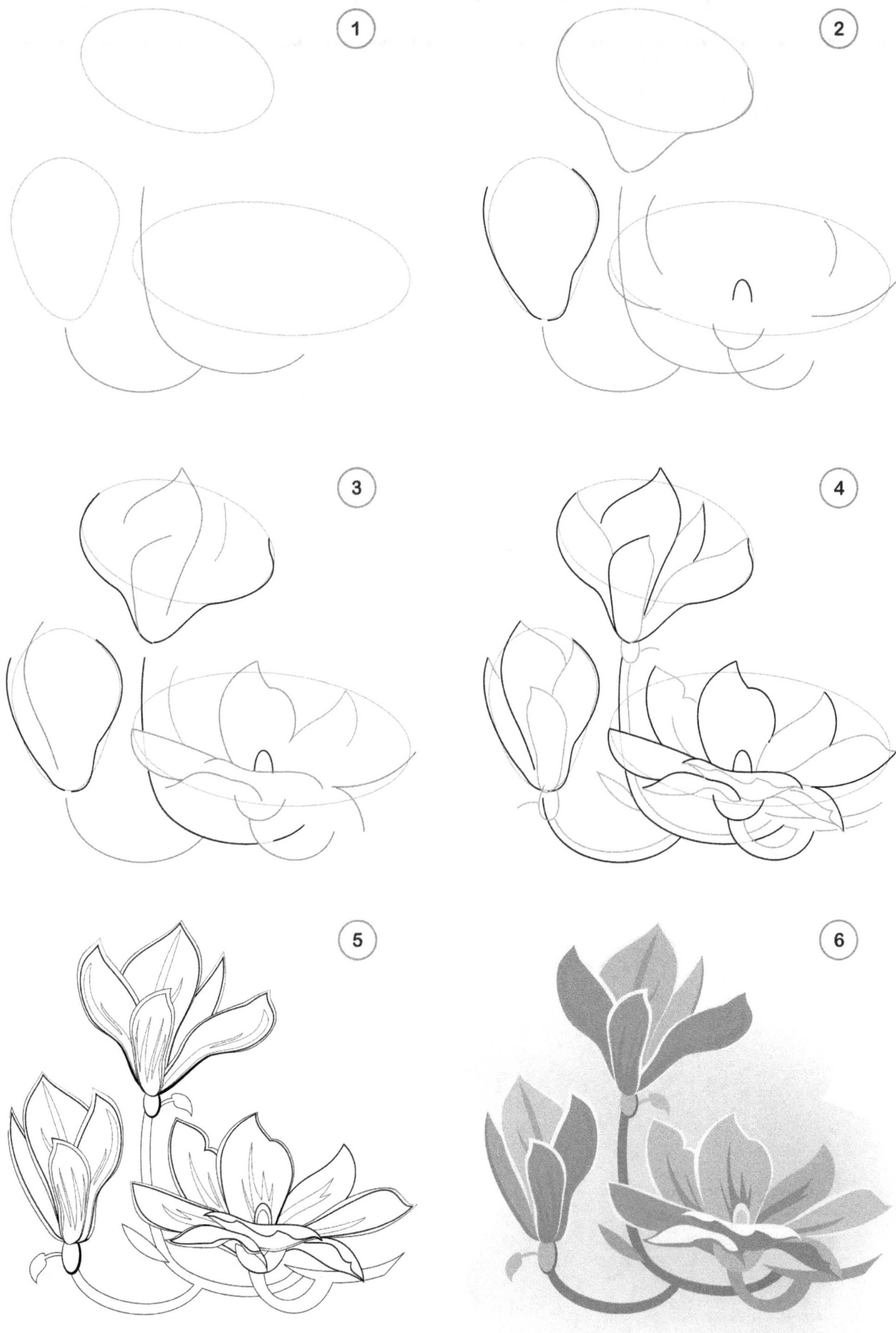

1
2
3
4
5
6

Your Turn to Draw

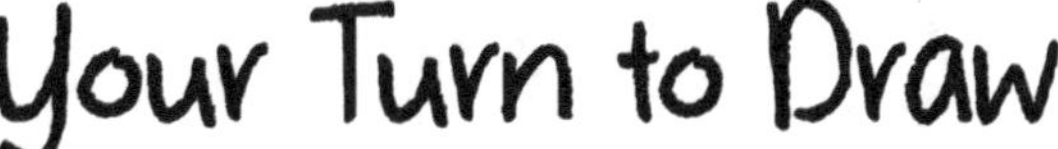

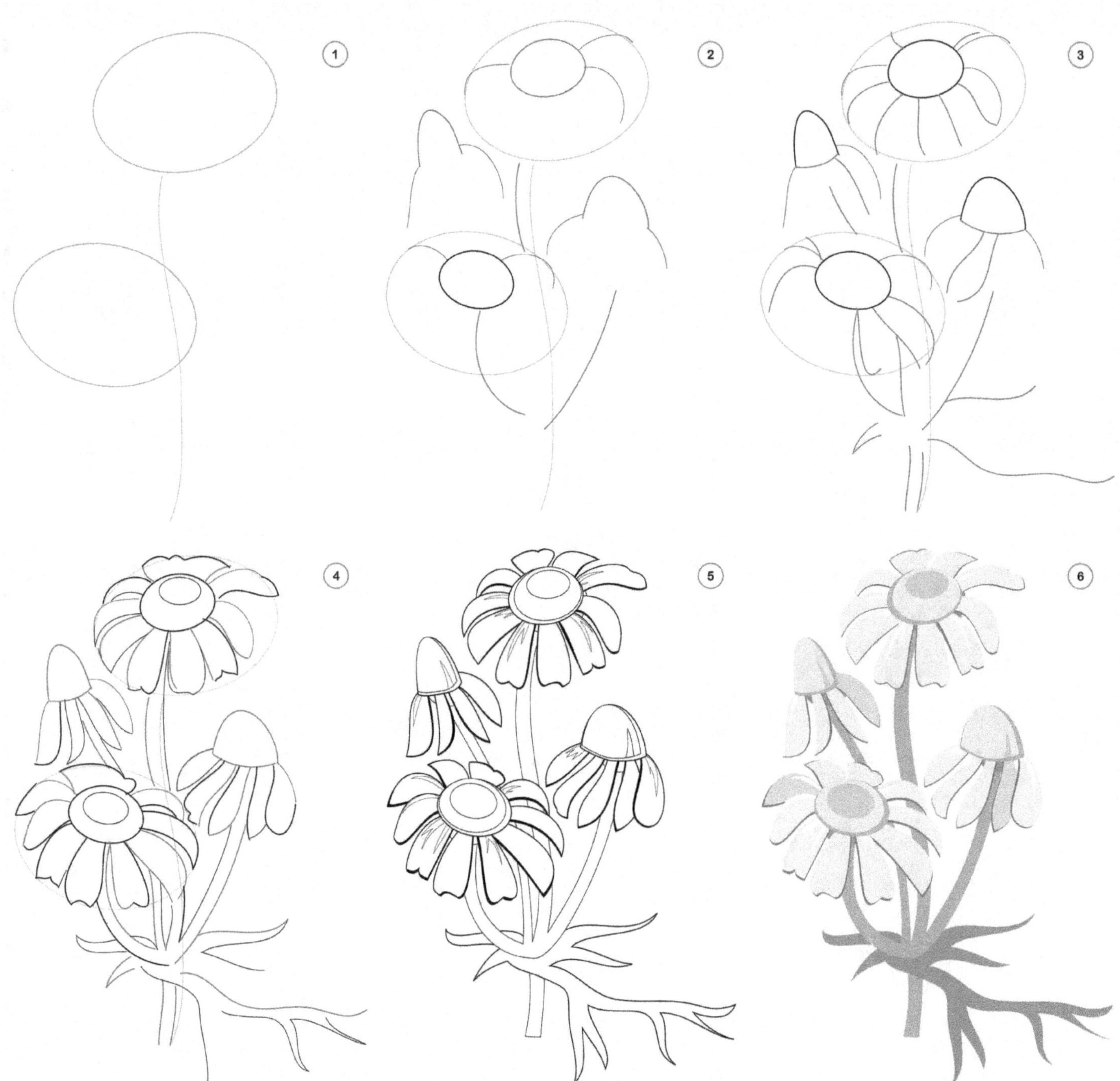

Your Turn to Draw

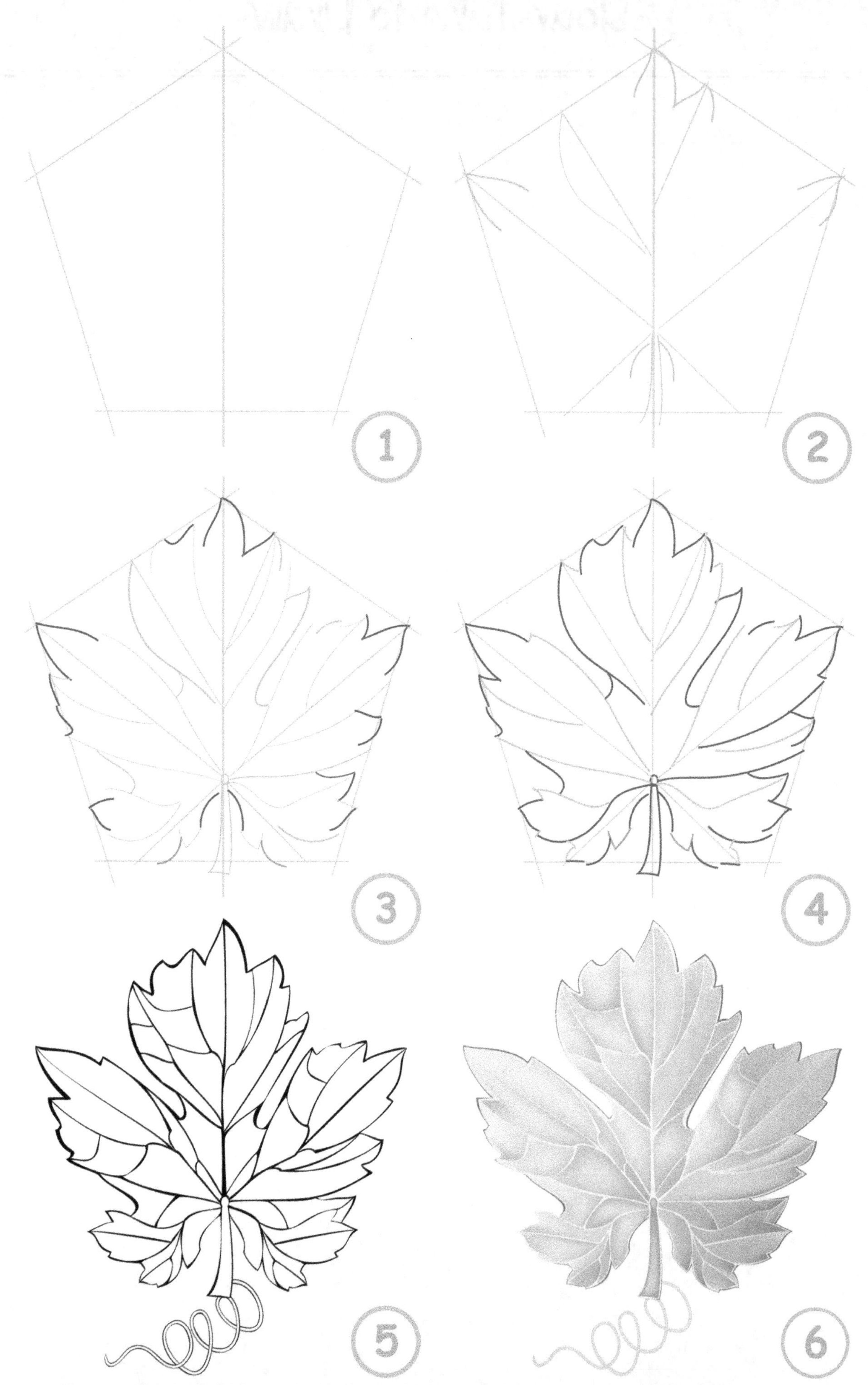

Your Turn to Draw

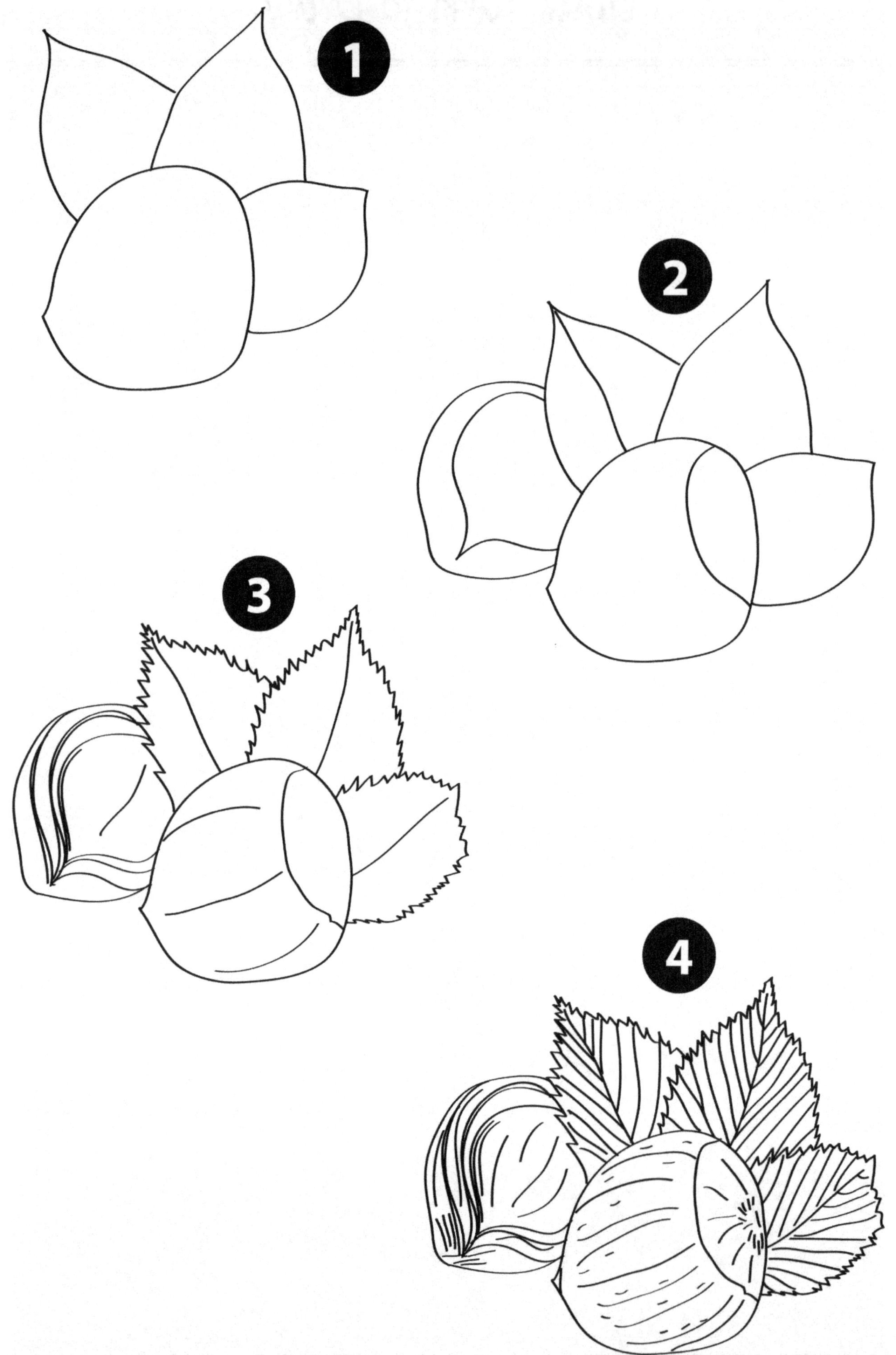

Your Turn to Draw

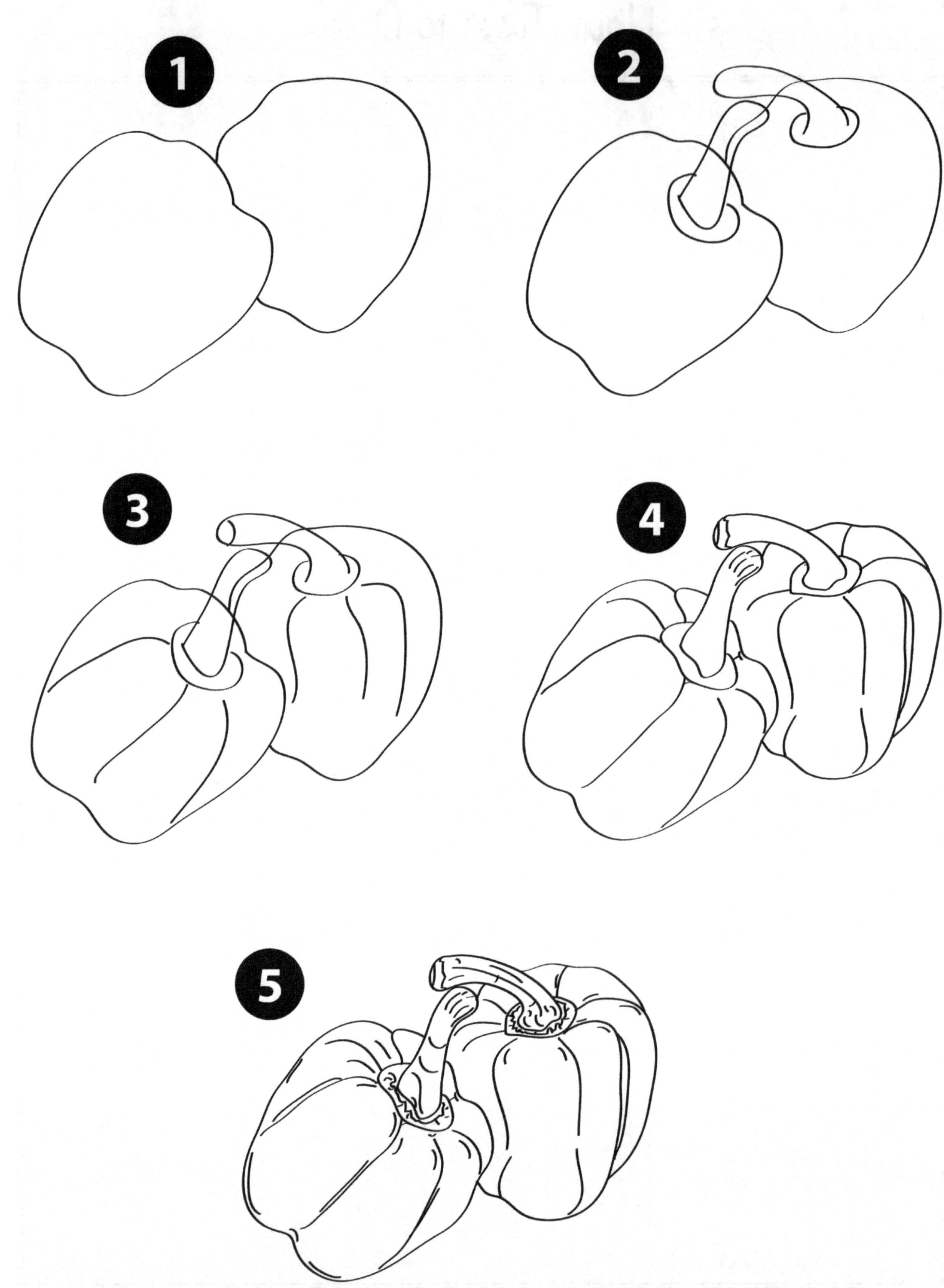

Your Turn to Draw

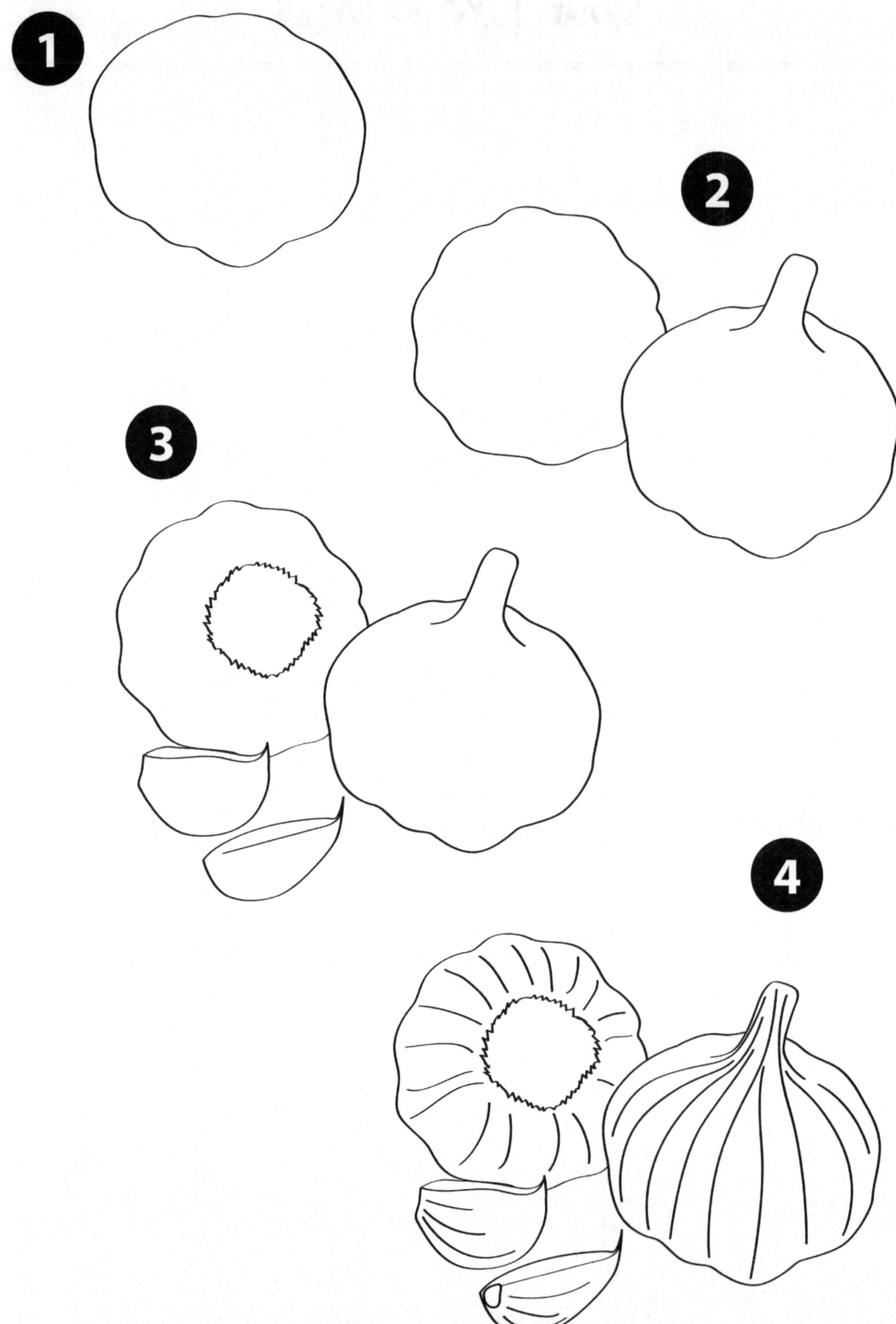

Your Turn to Draw

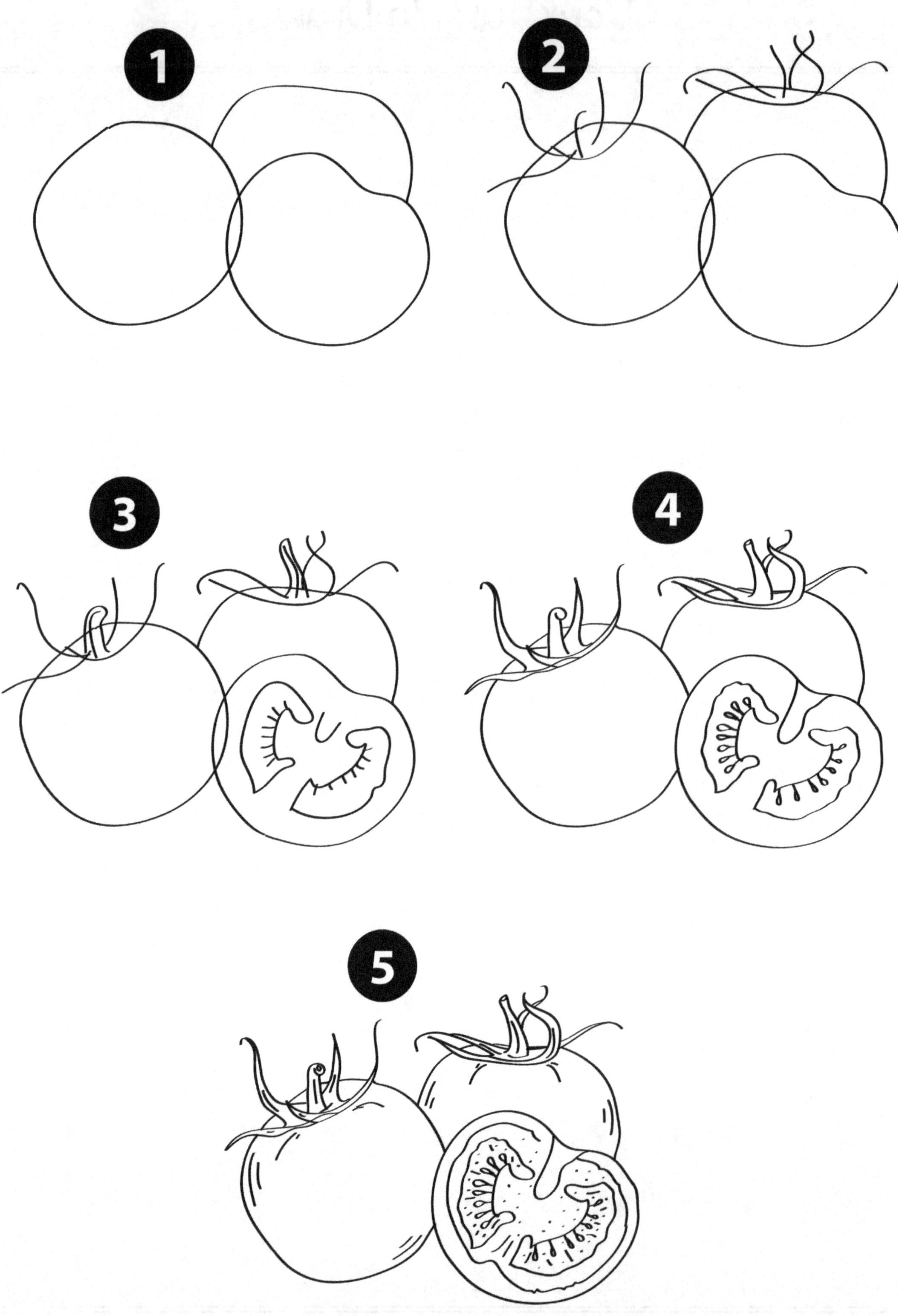

Your Turn to Draw

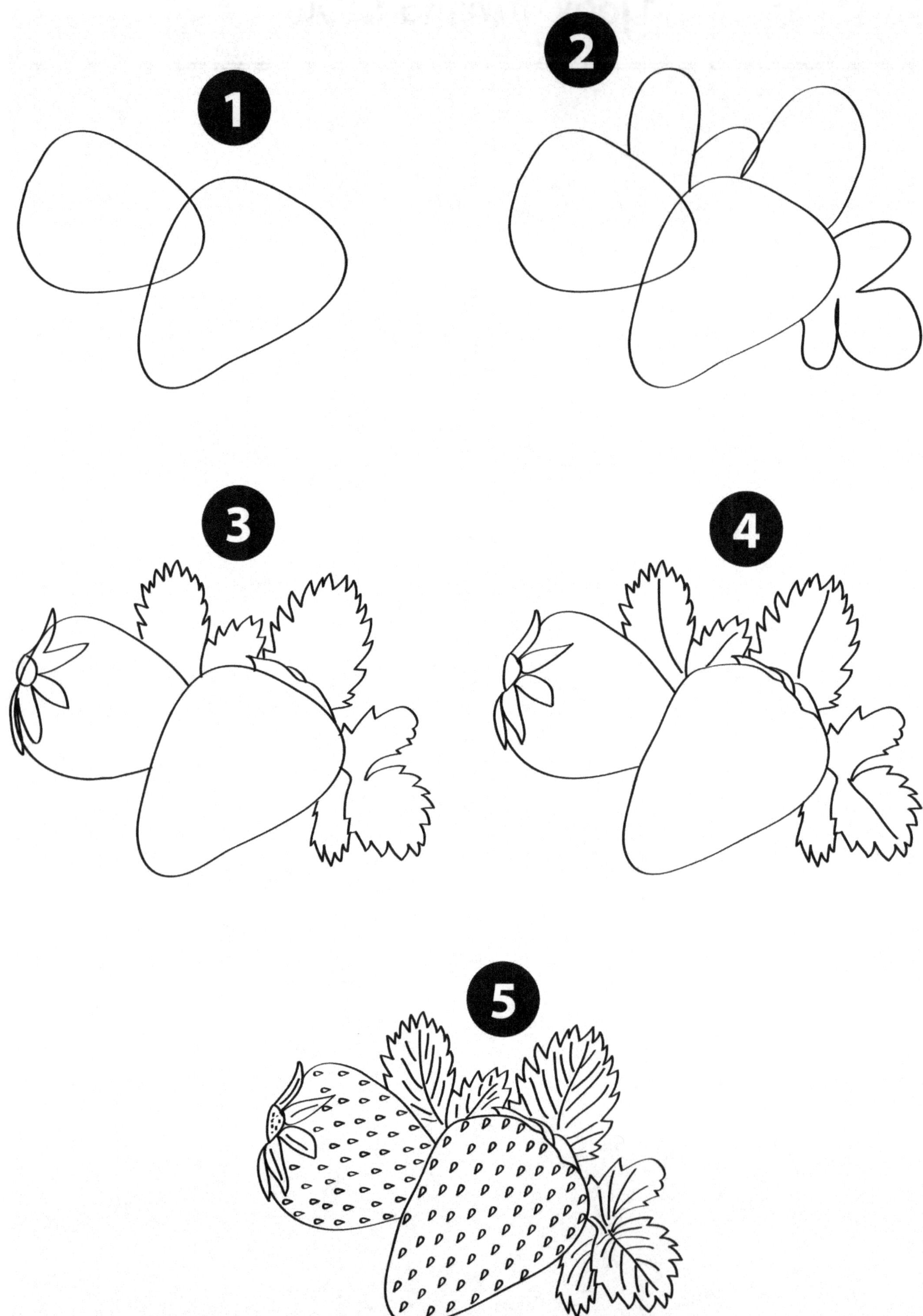

Your Turn to Draw

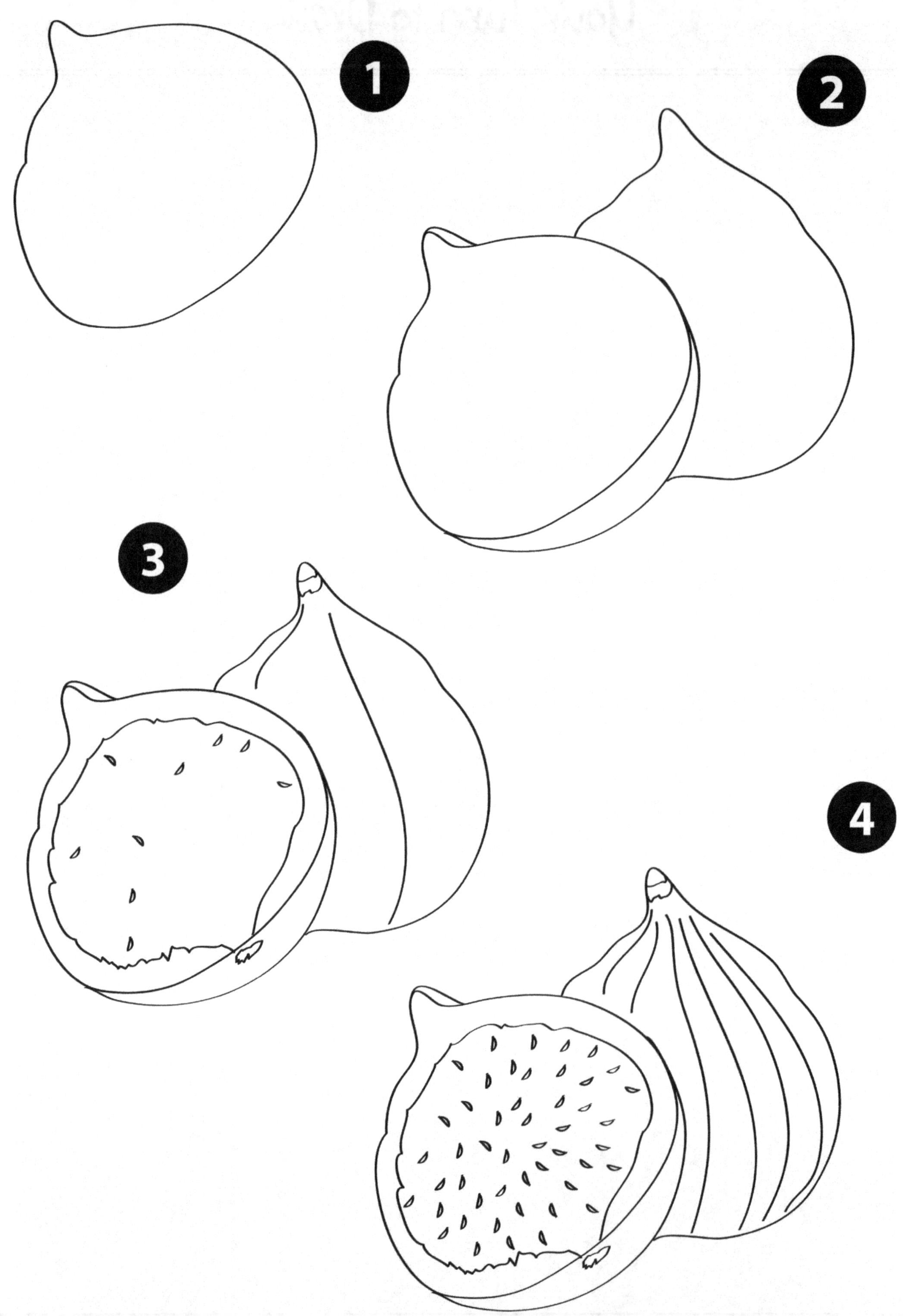

Your Turn to Draw

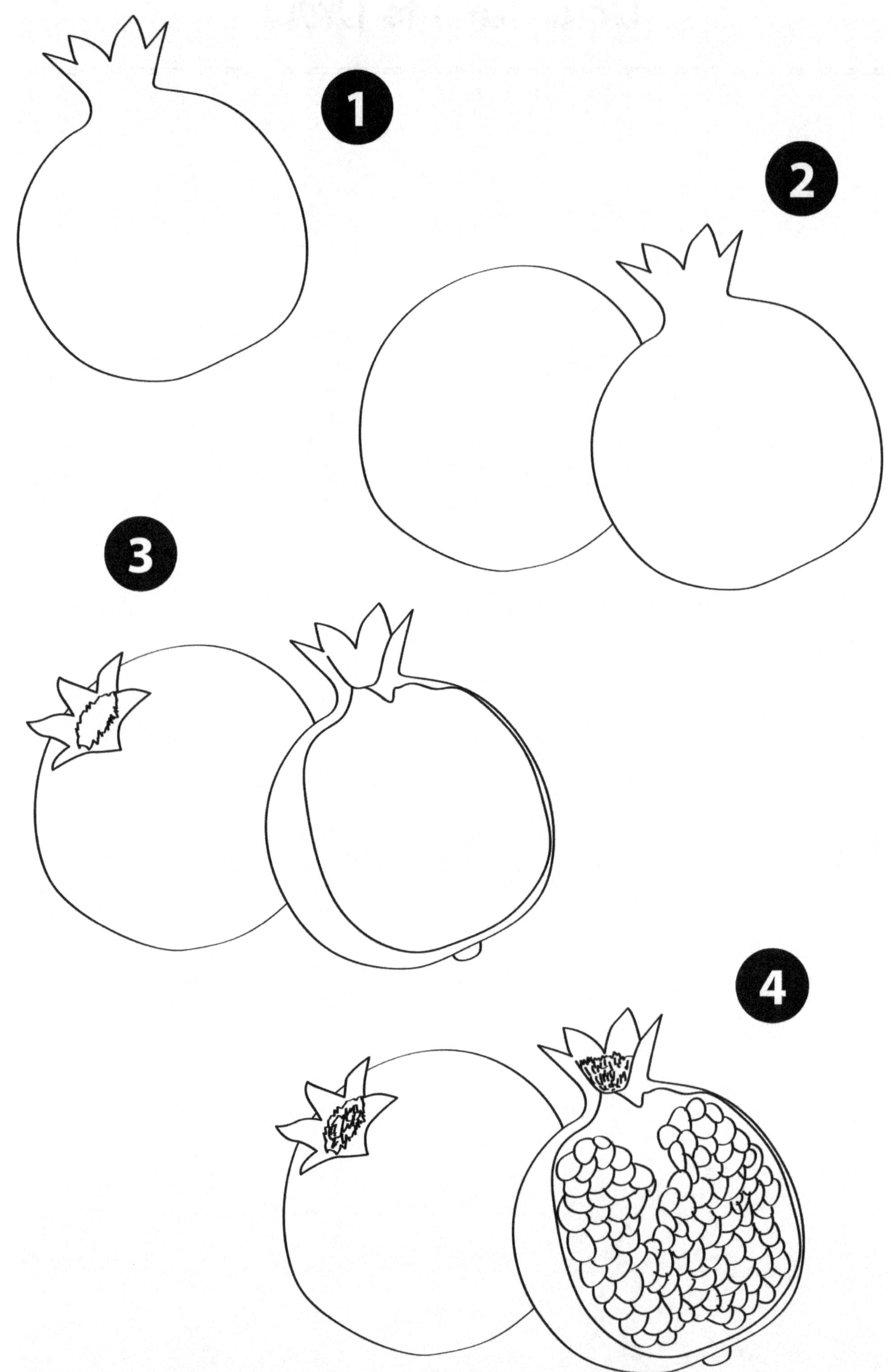
1
2
3
4

Your Turn to Draw

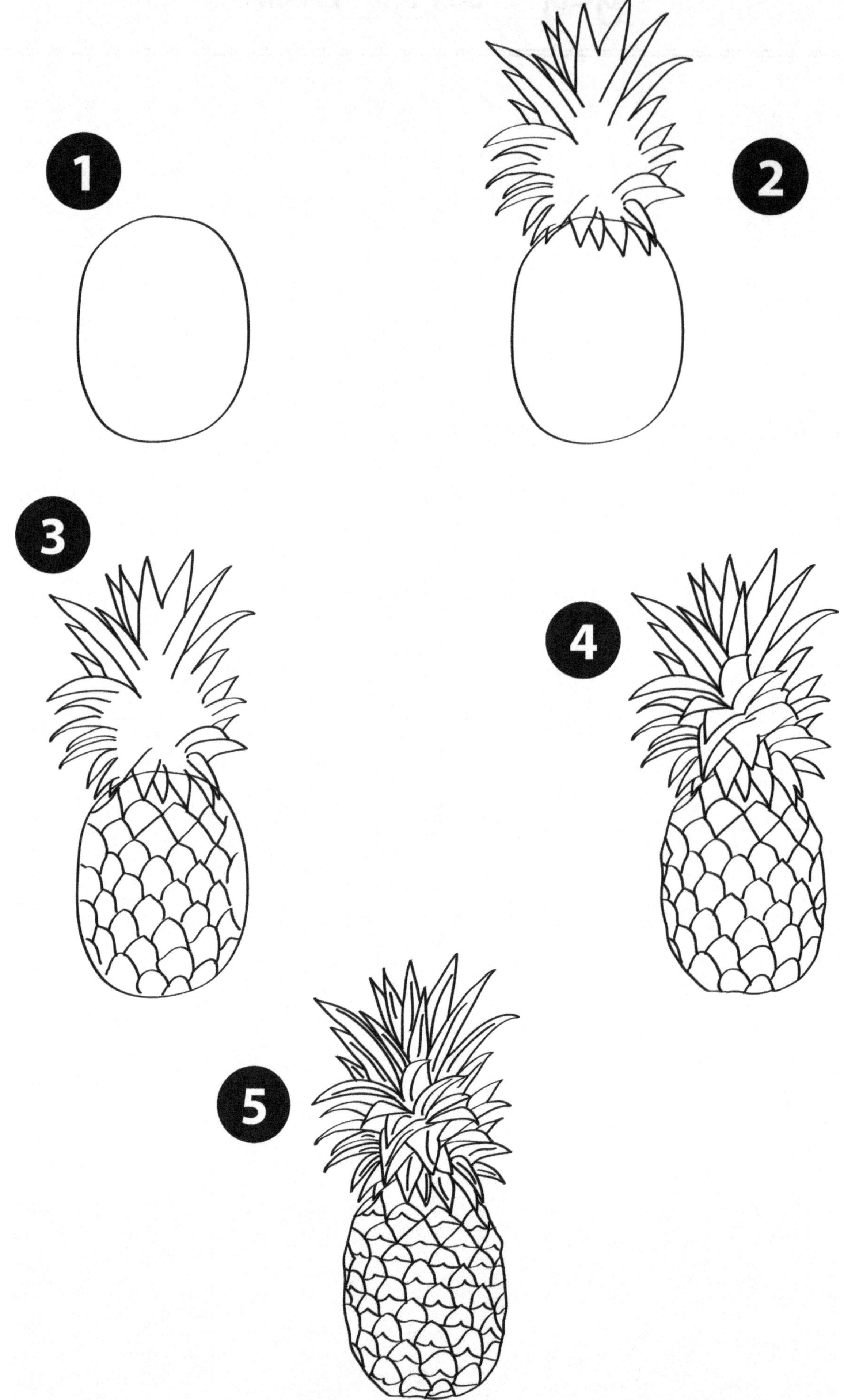

1
2
3
4
5

Your Turn to Draw

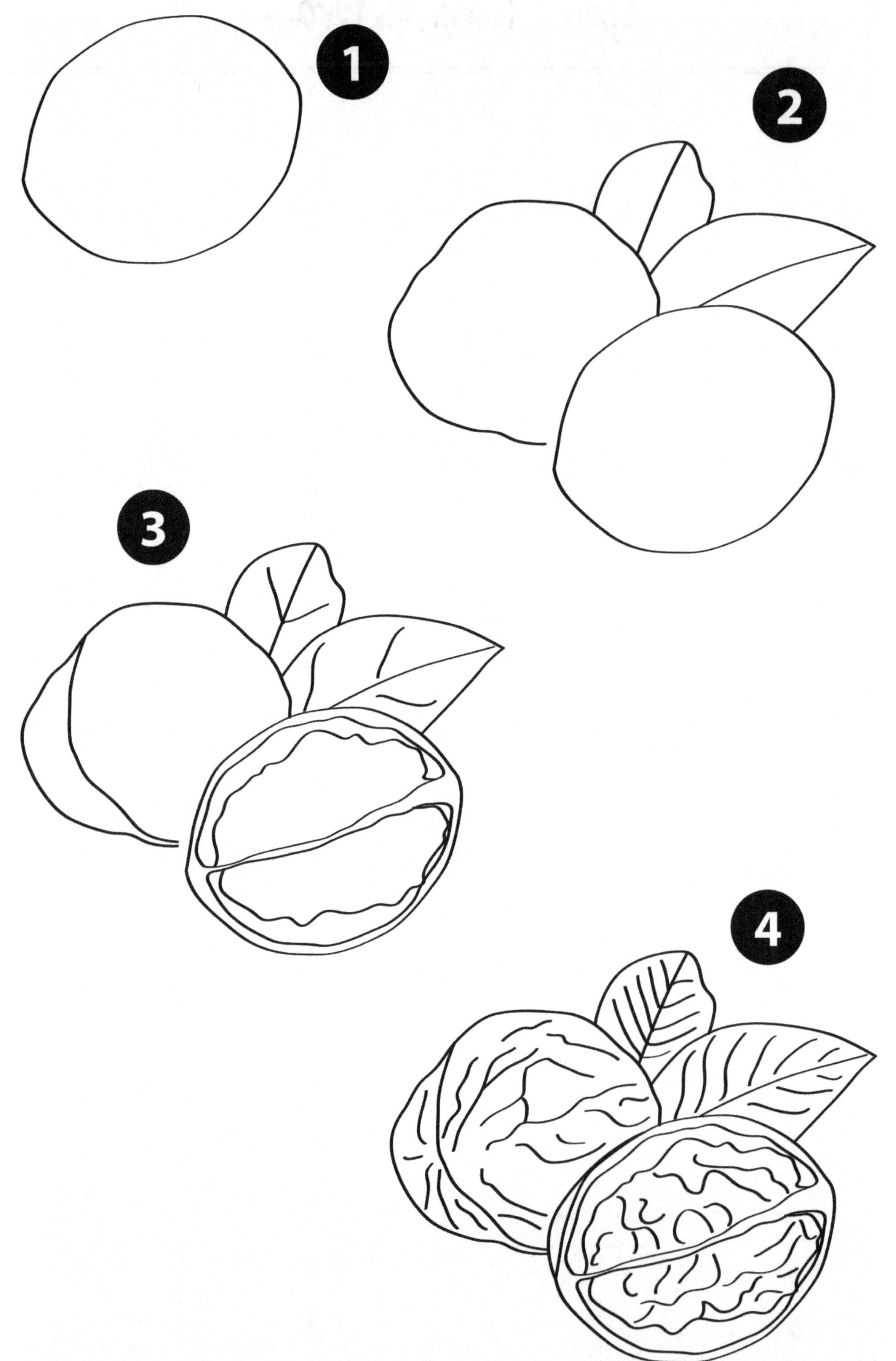

Your Turn to Draw

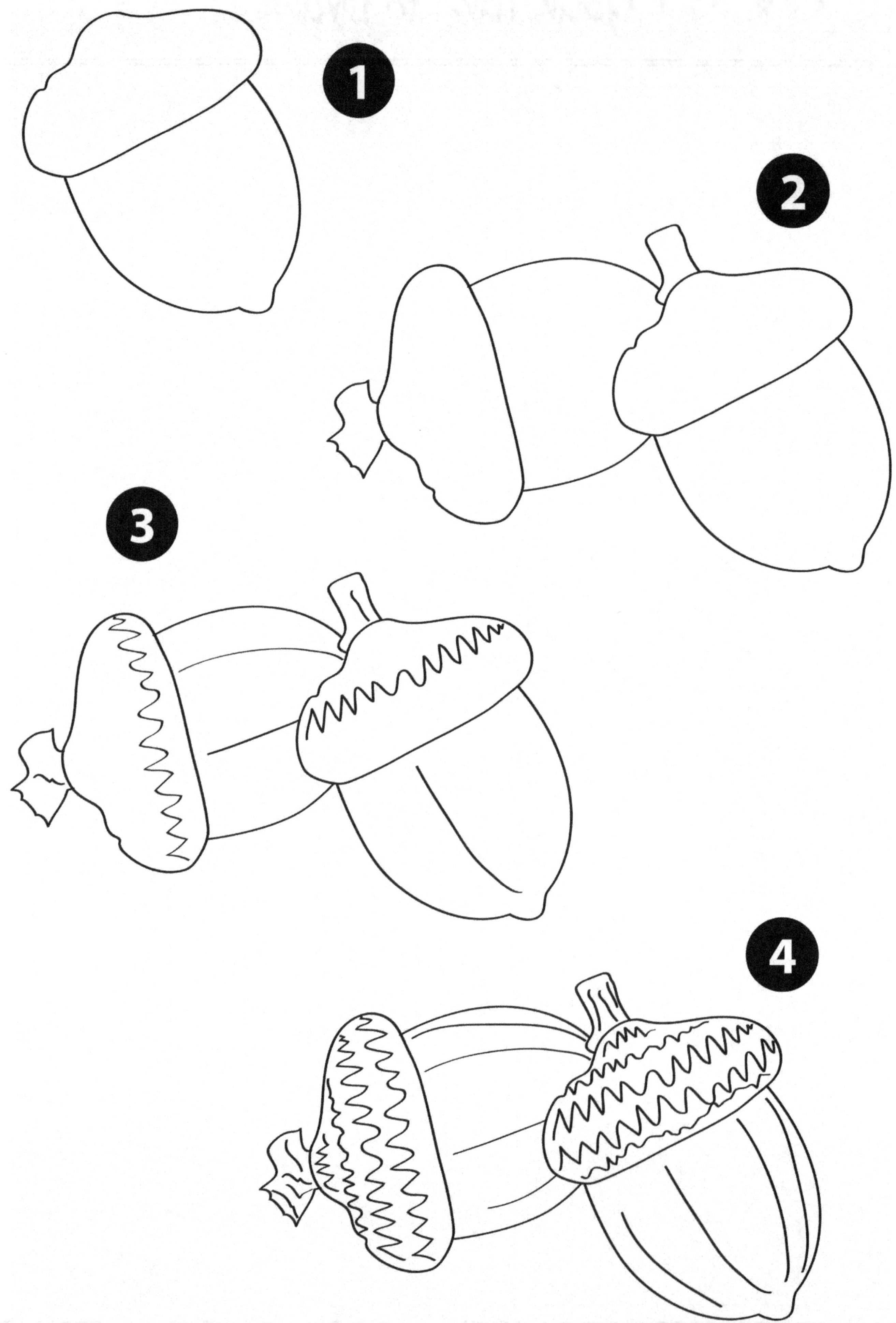

Your Turn to Draw

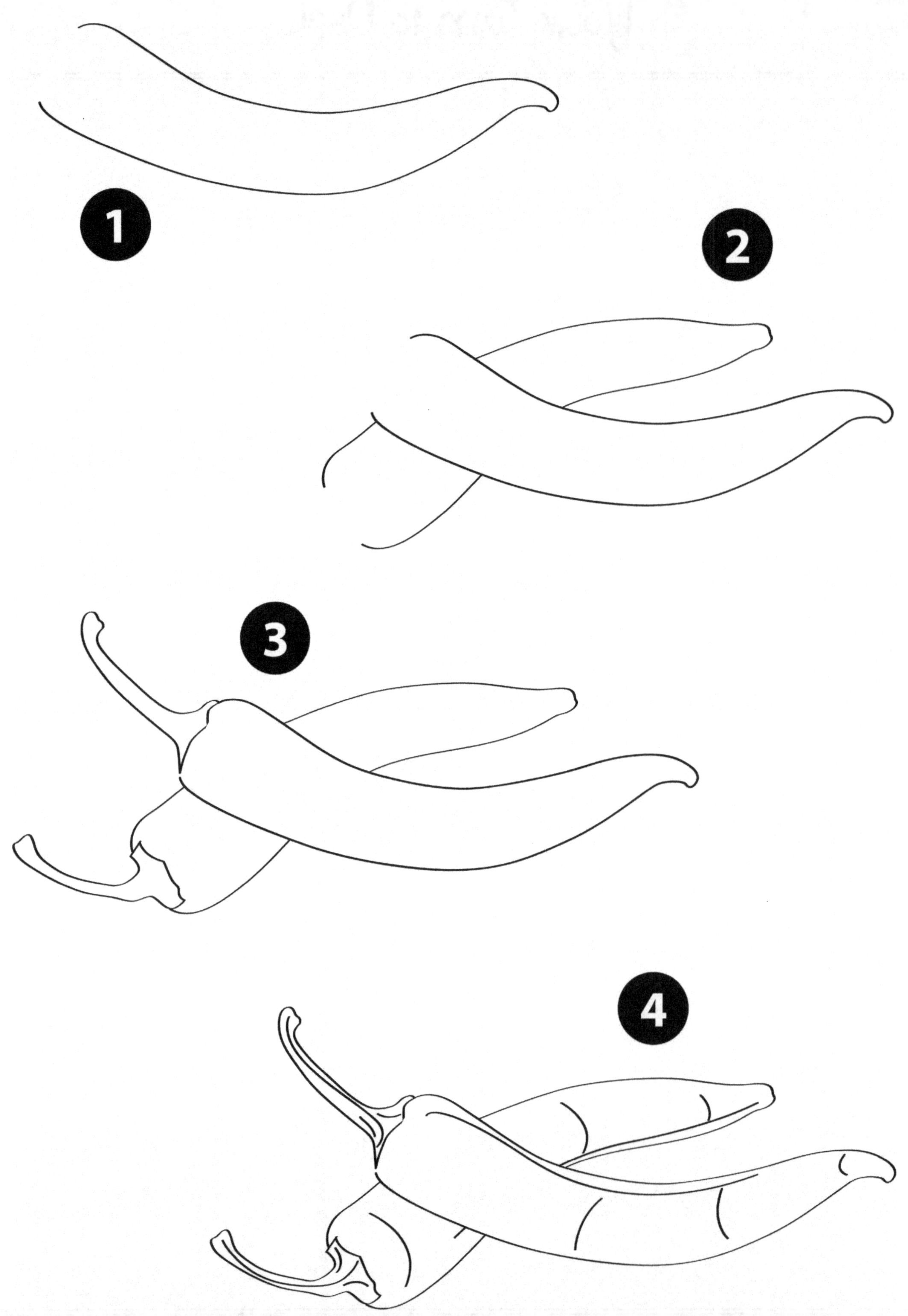

Your Turn to Draw

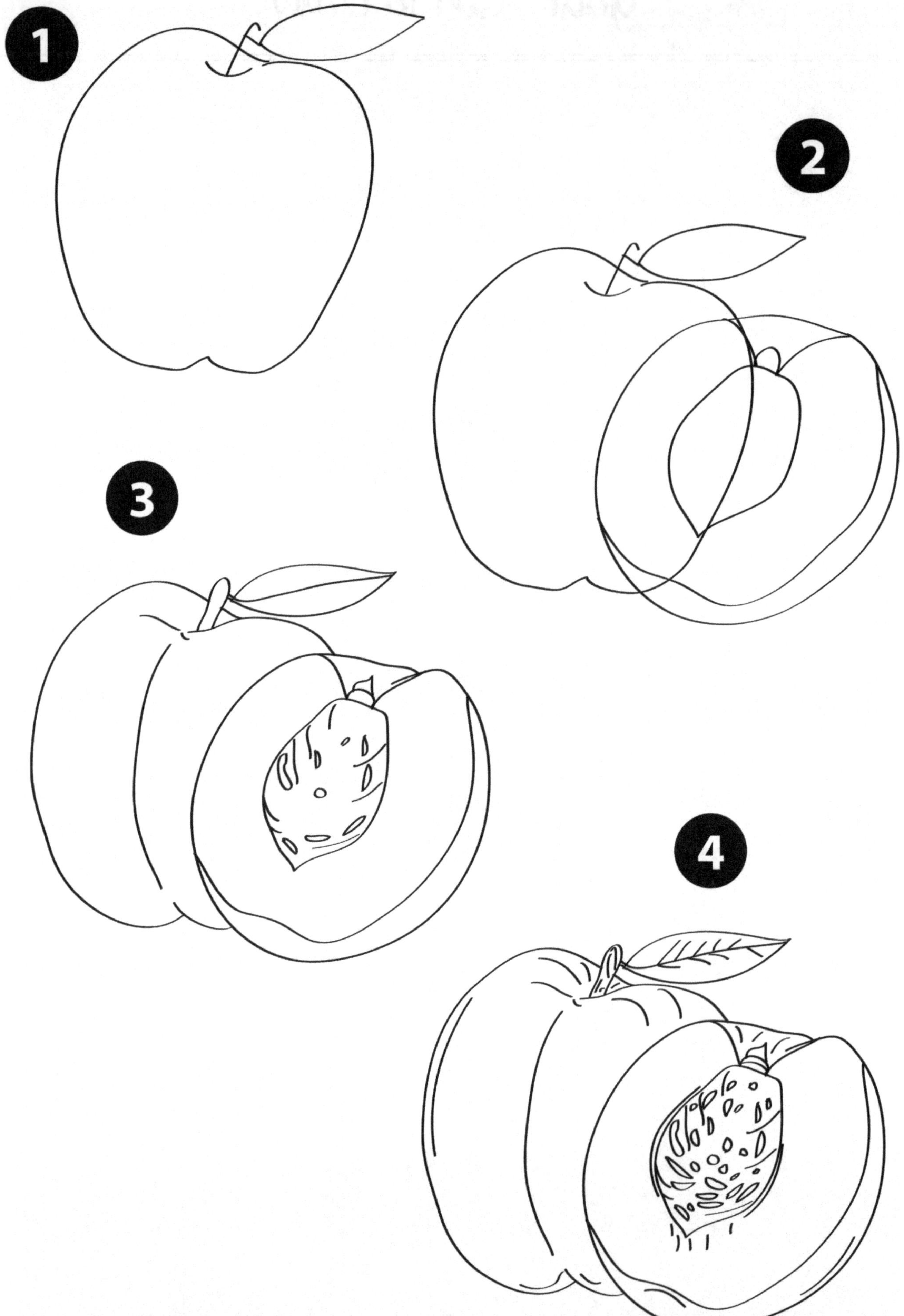

1
2
3
4

Your Turn to Draw

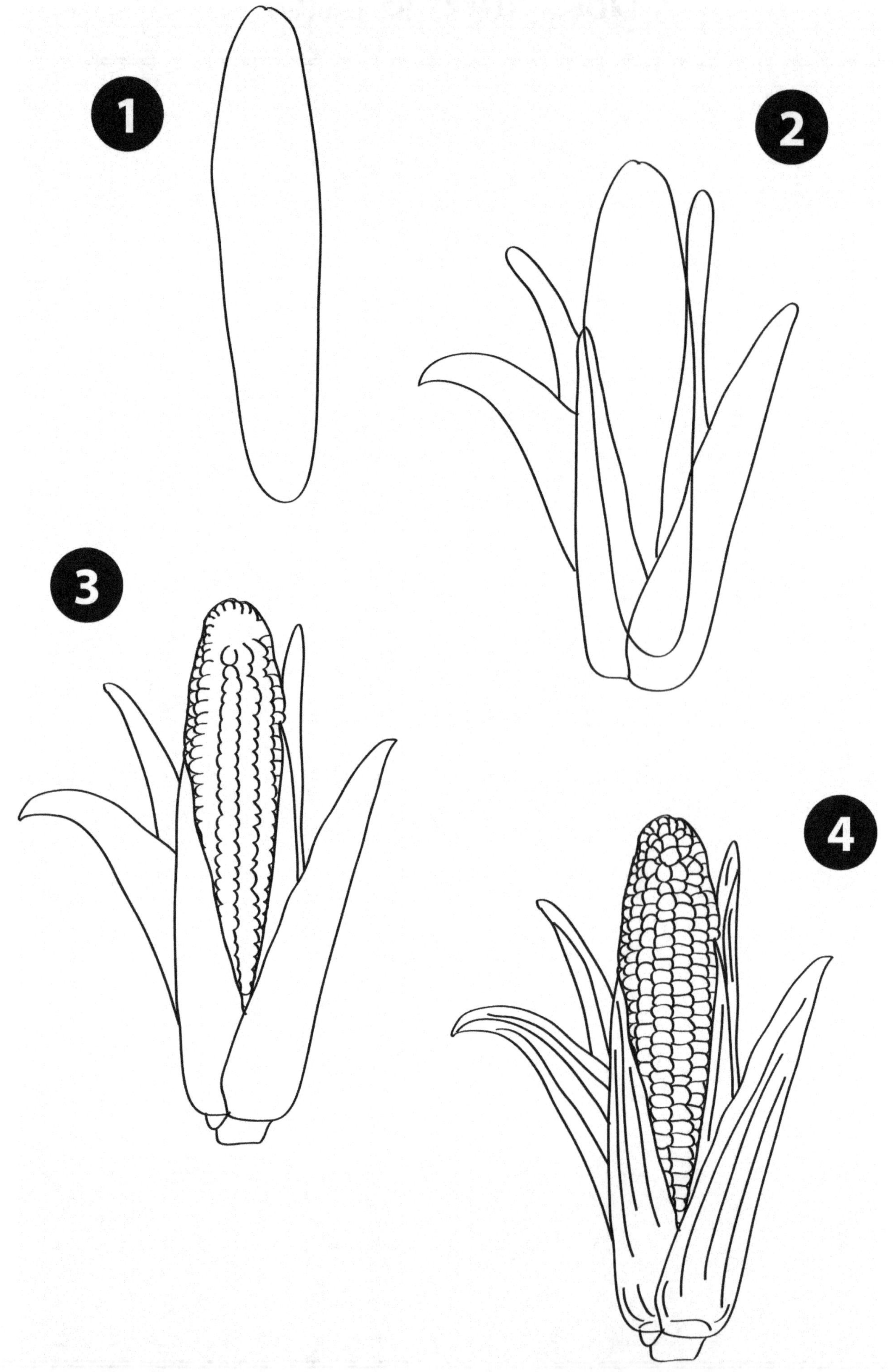

Your Turn to Draw

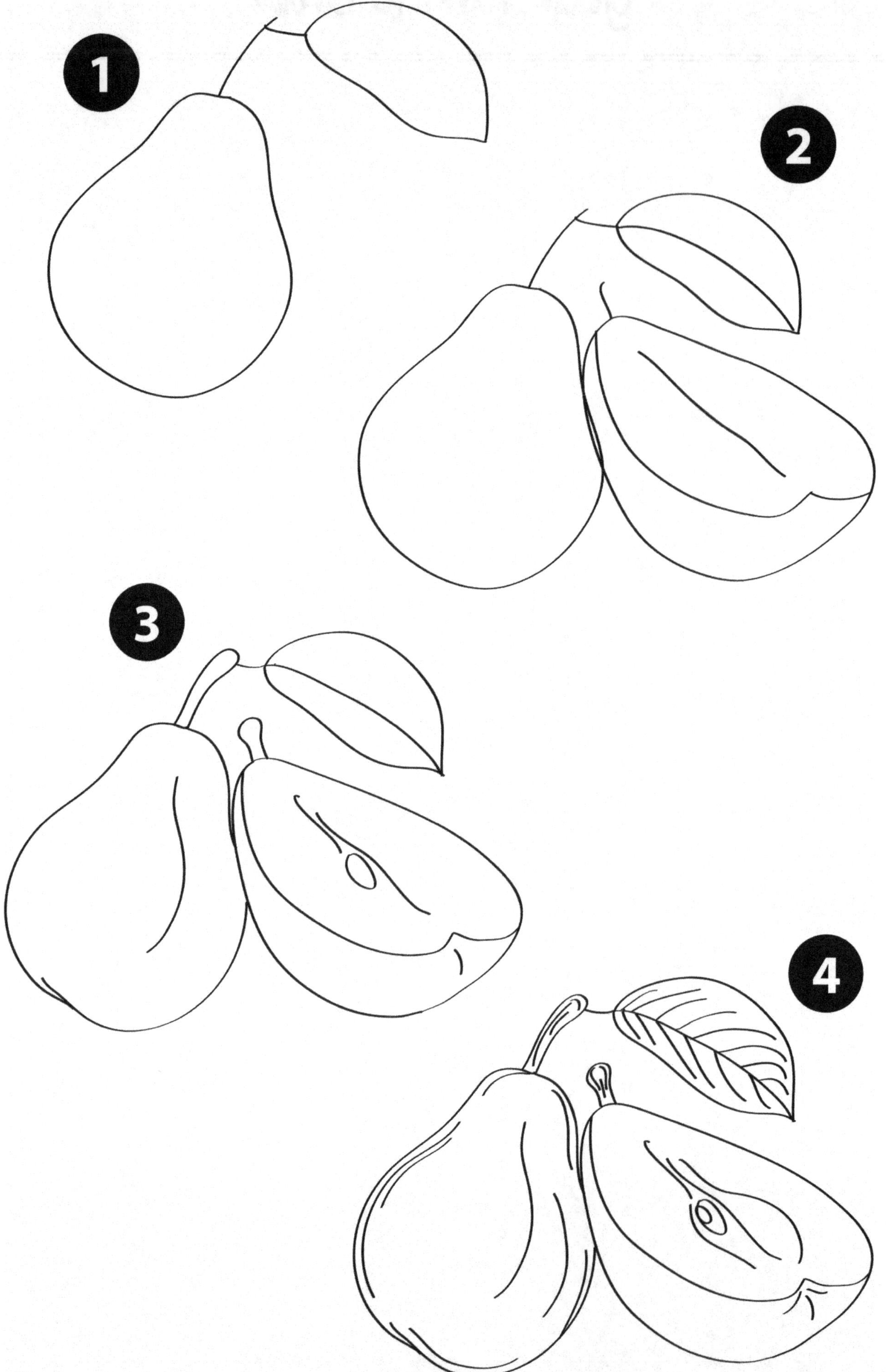

Your Turn to Draw

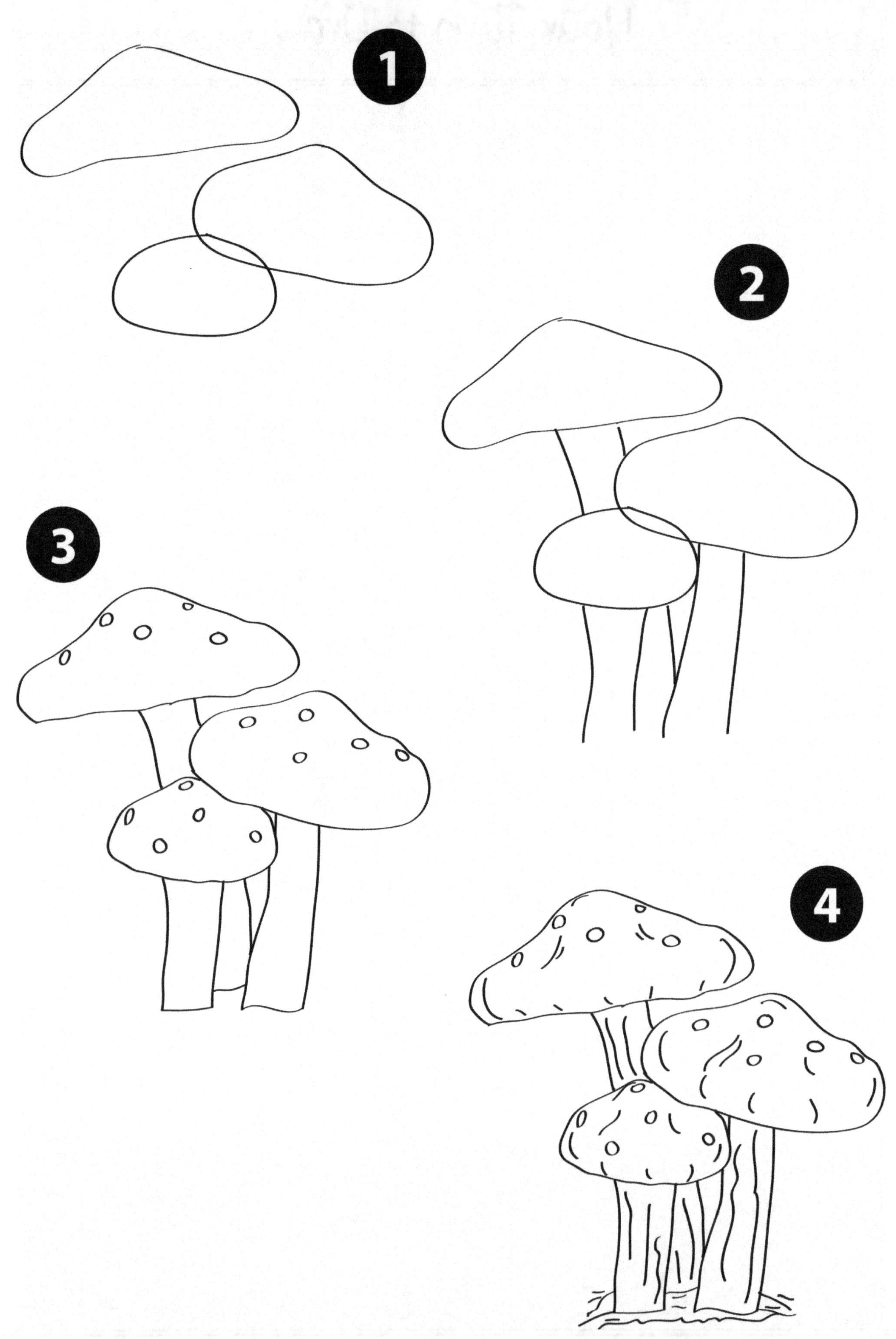

Your Turn to Draw

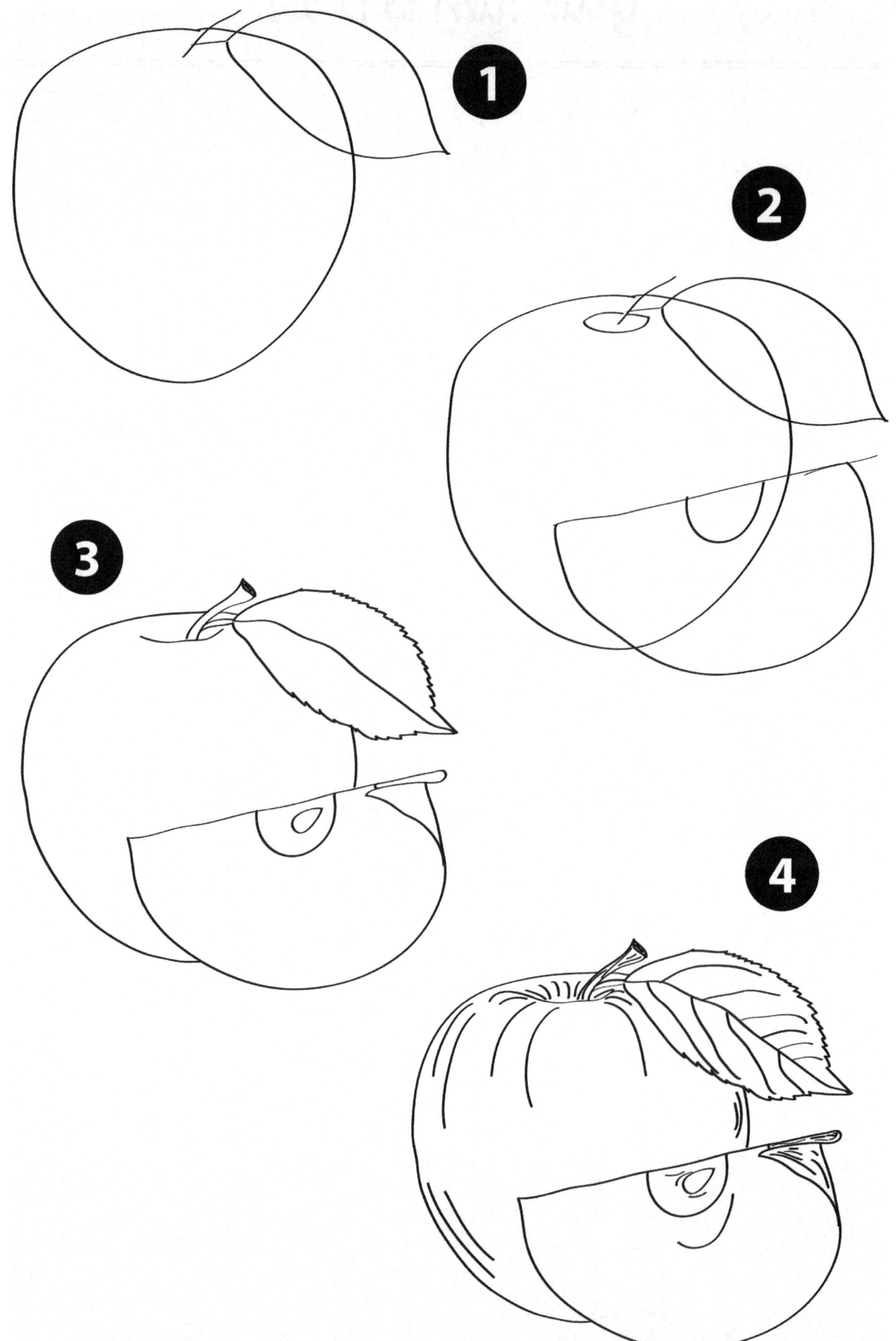

Your Turn to Draw

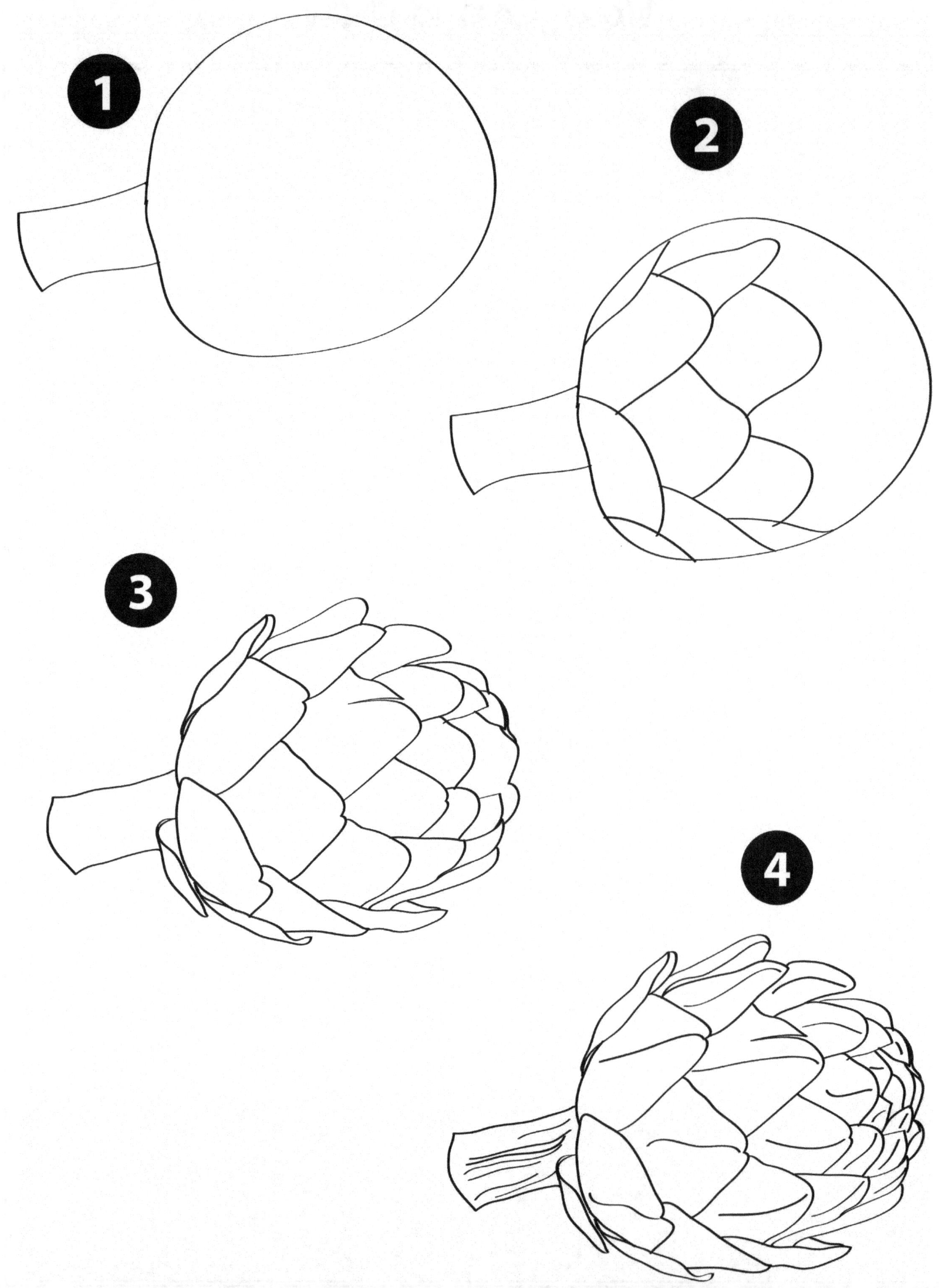

Your Turn to Draw

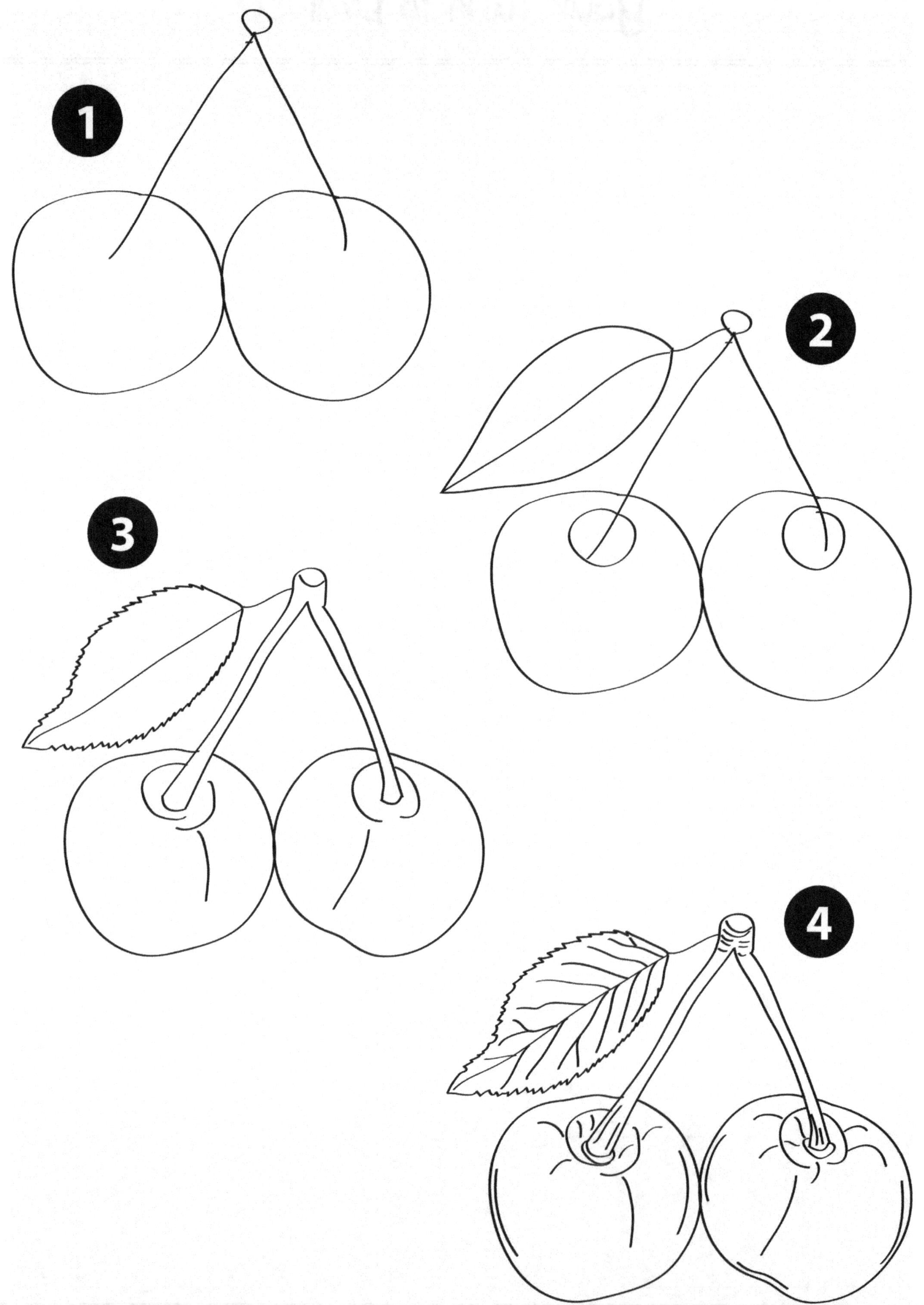

1
2
3
4

Your Turn to Draw

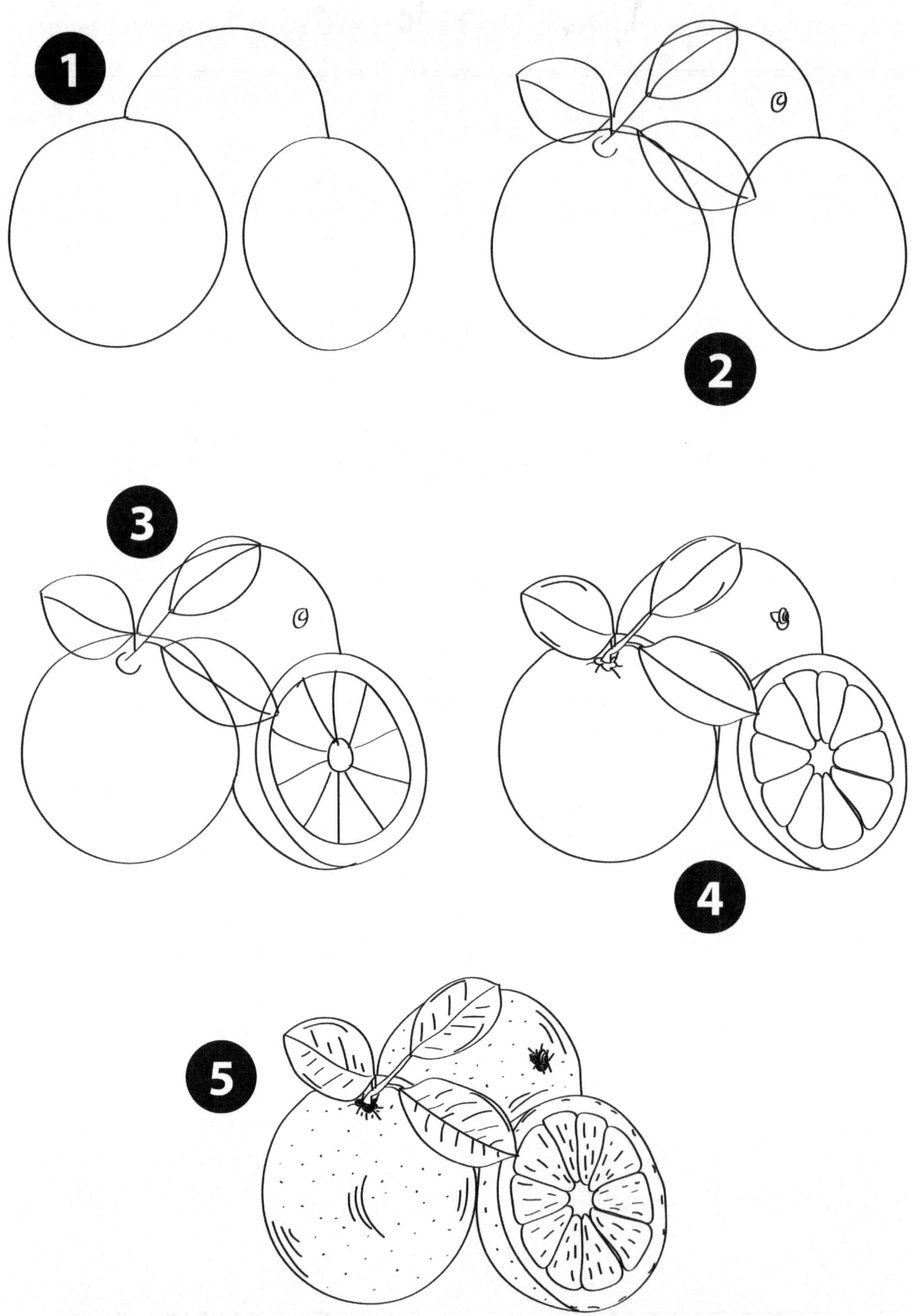

Your Turn to Draw

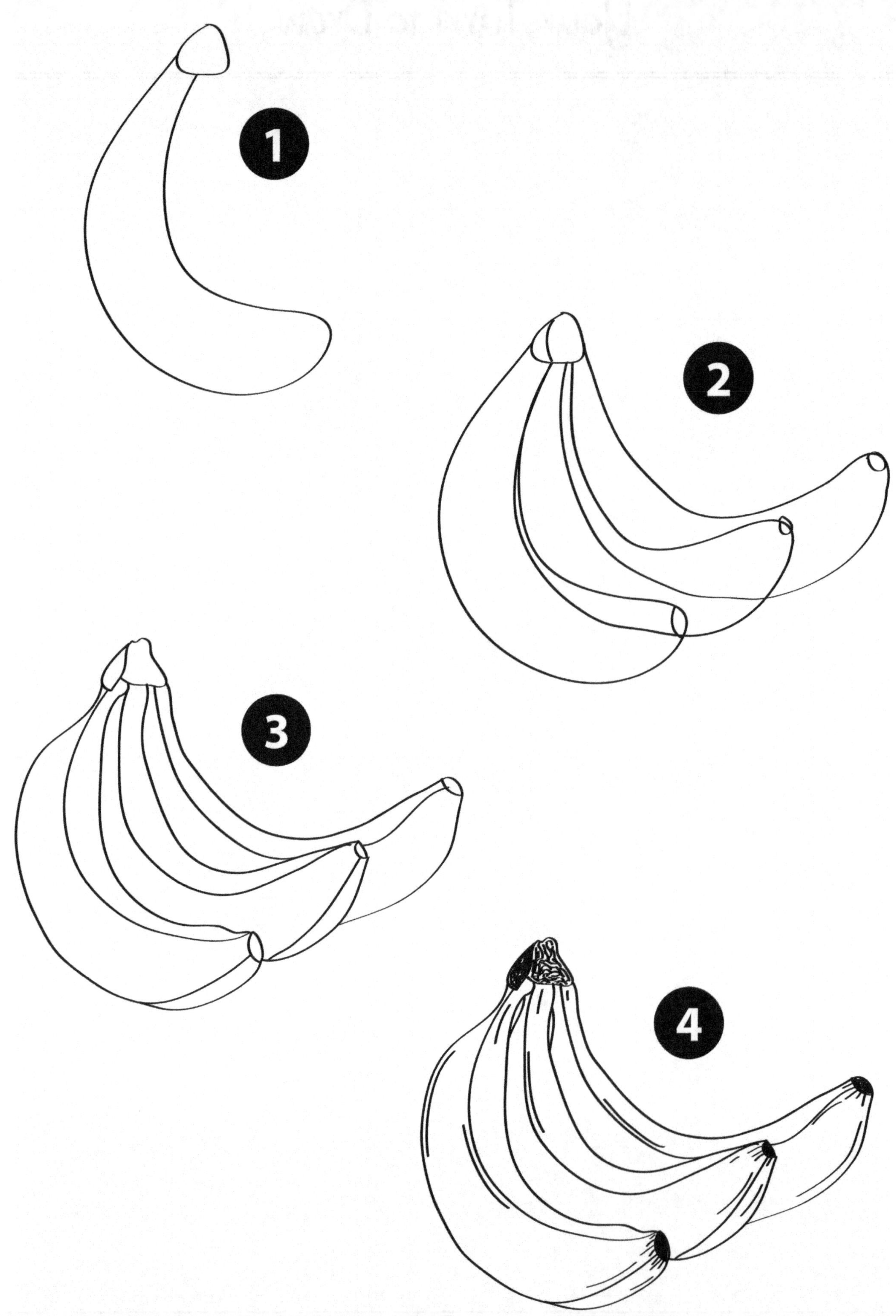

Your Turn to Draw

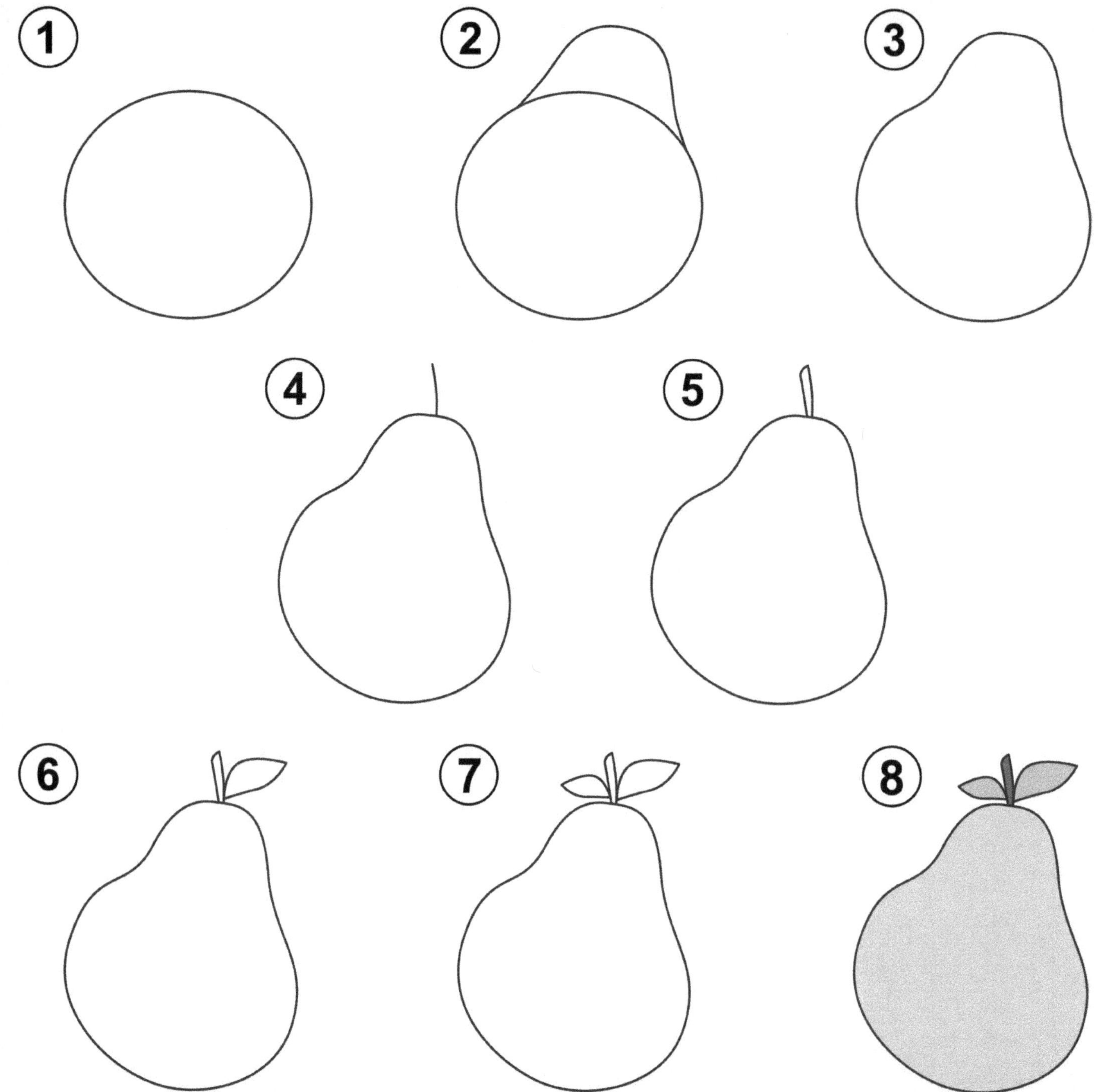

1
2
3
4
5
6
7
8

Your Turn to Draw

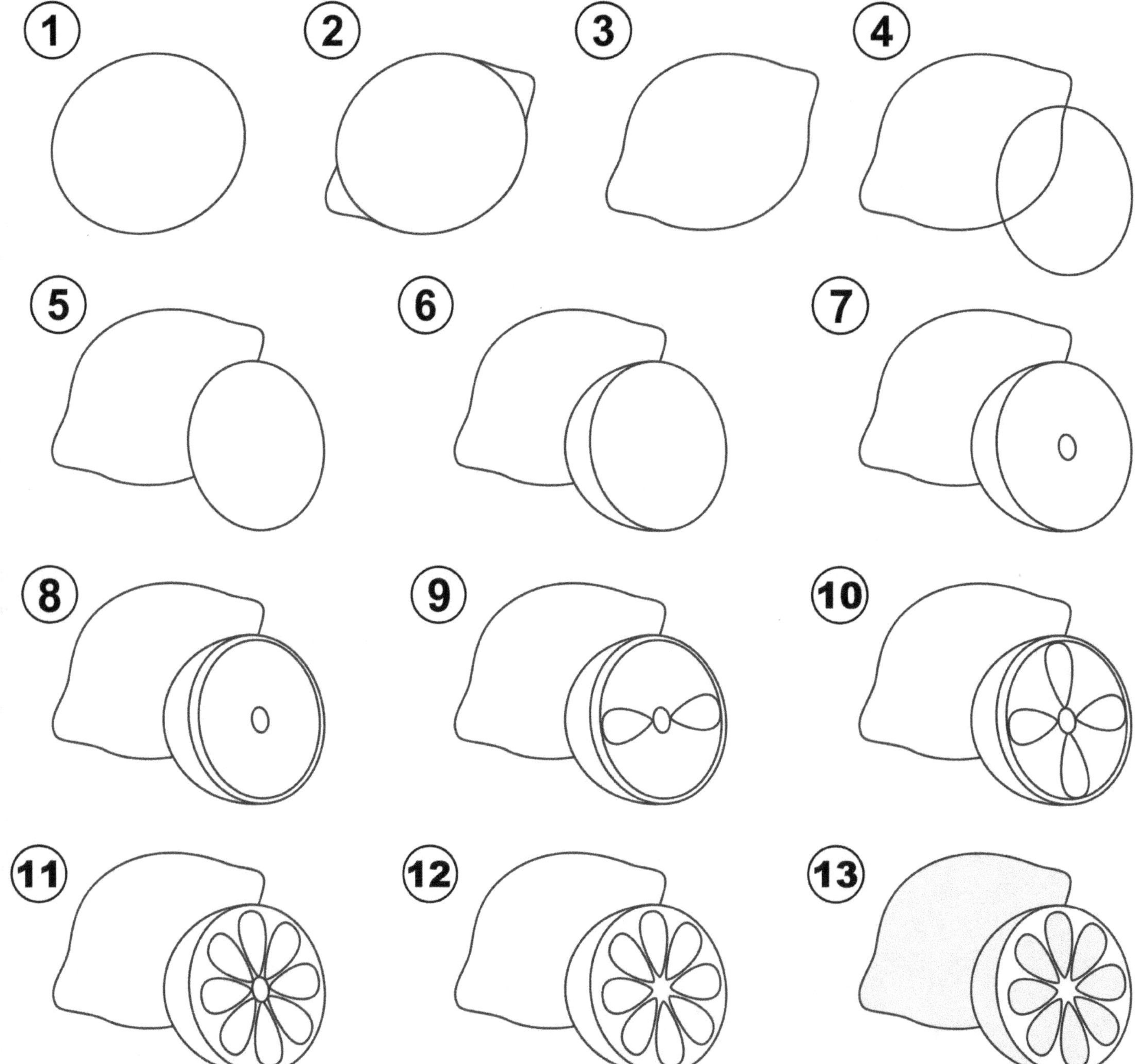

Your Turn to Draw

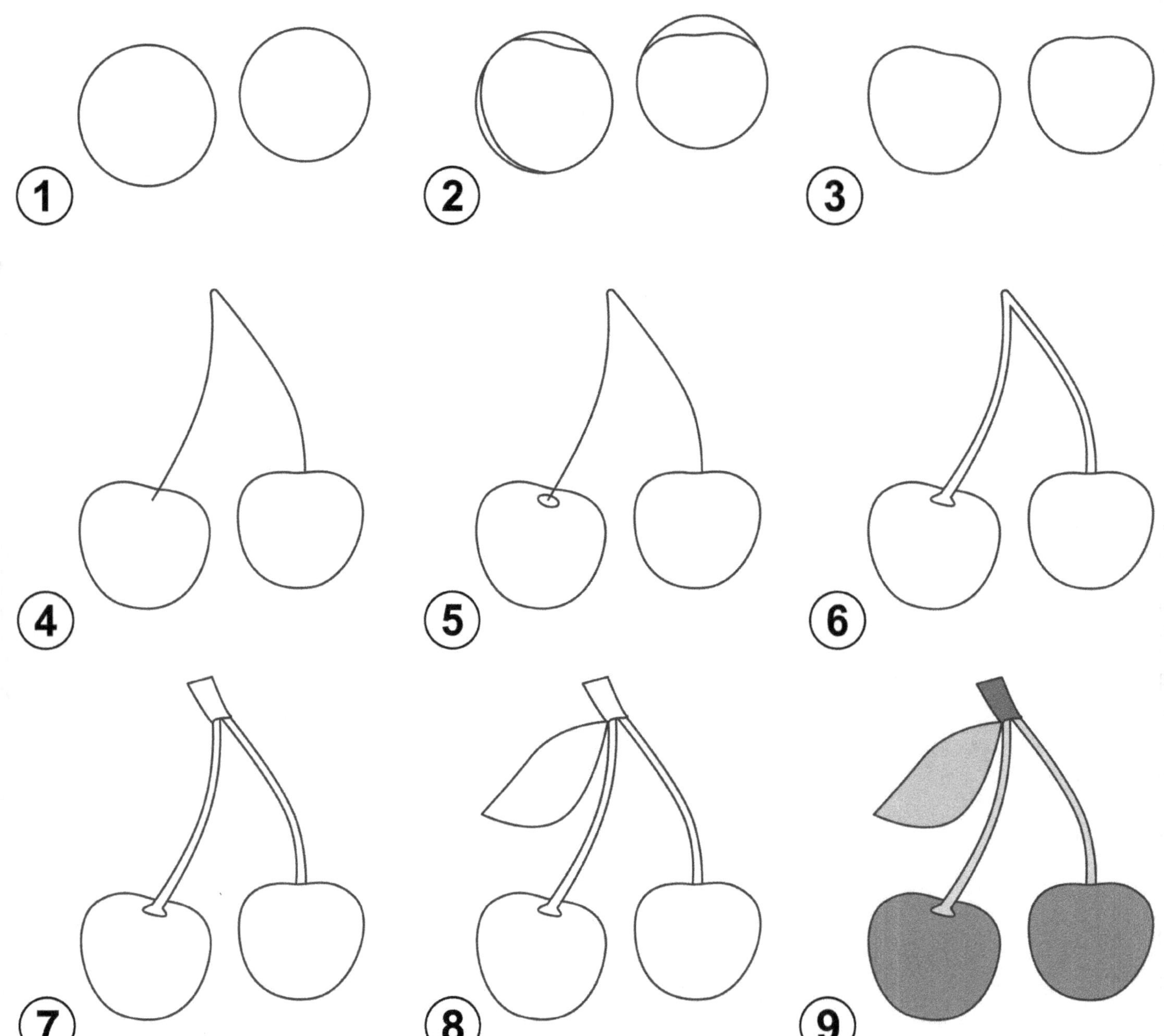

Your Turn to Draw

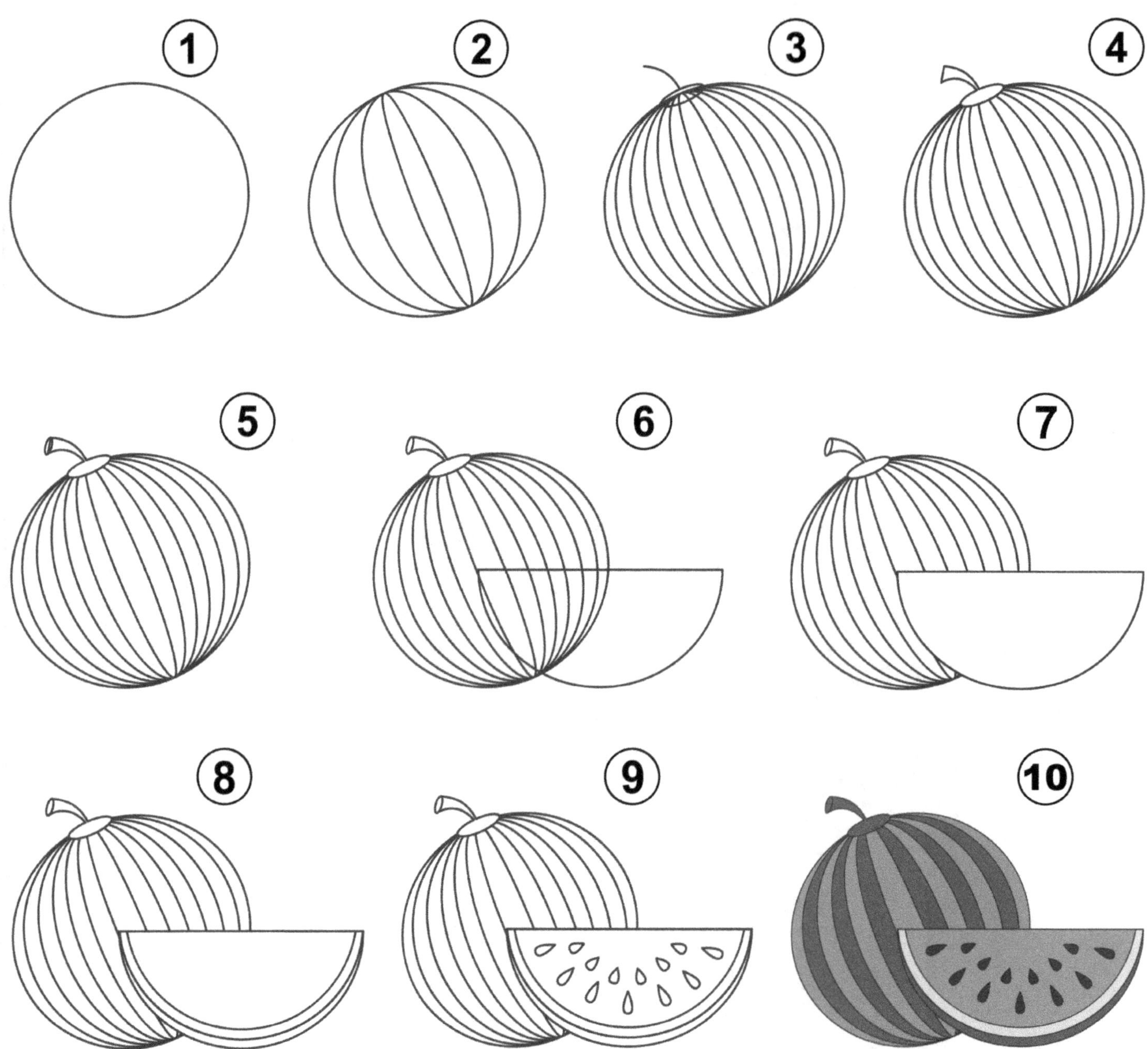

Your Turn to Draw

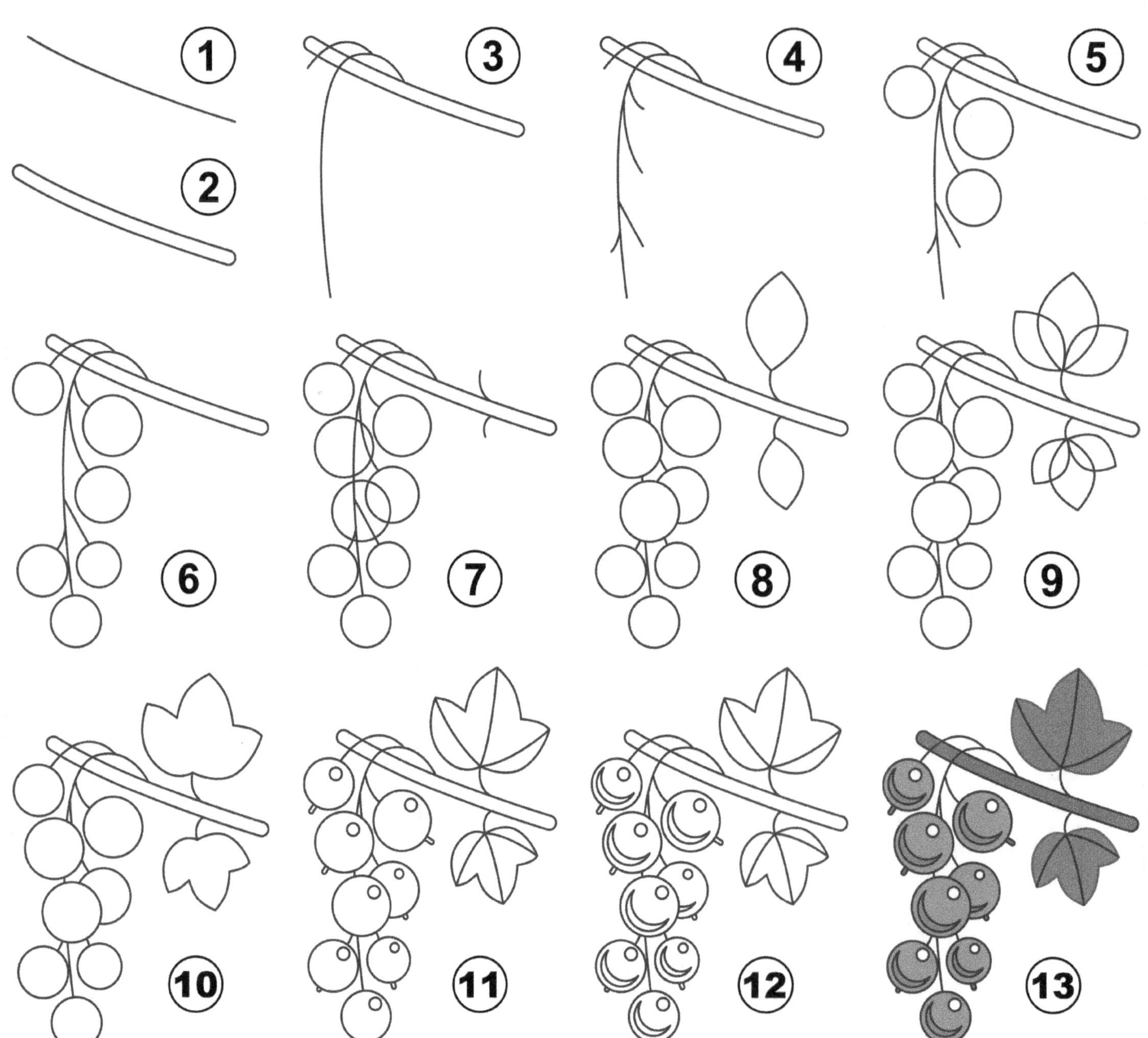

Your Turn to Draw

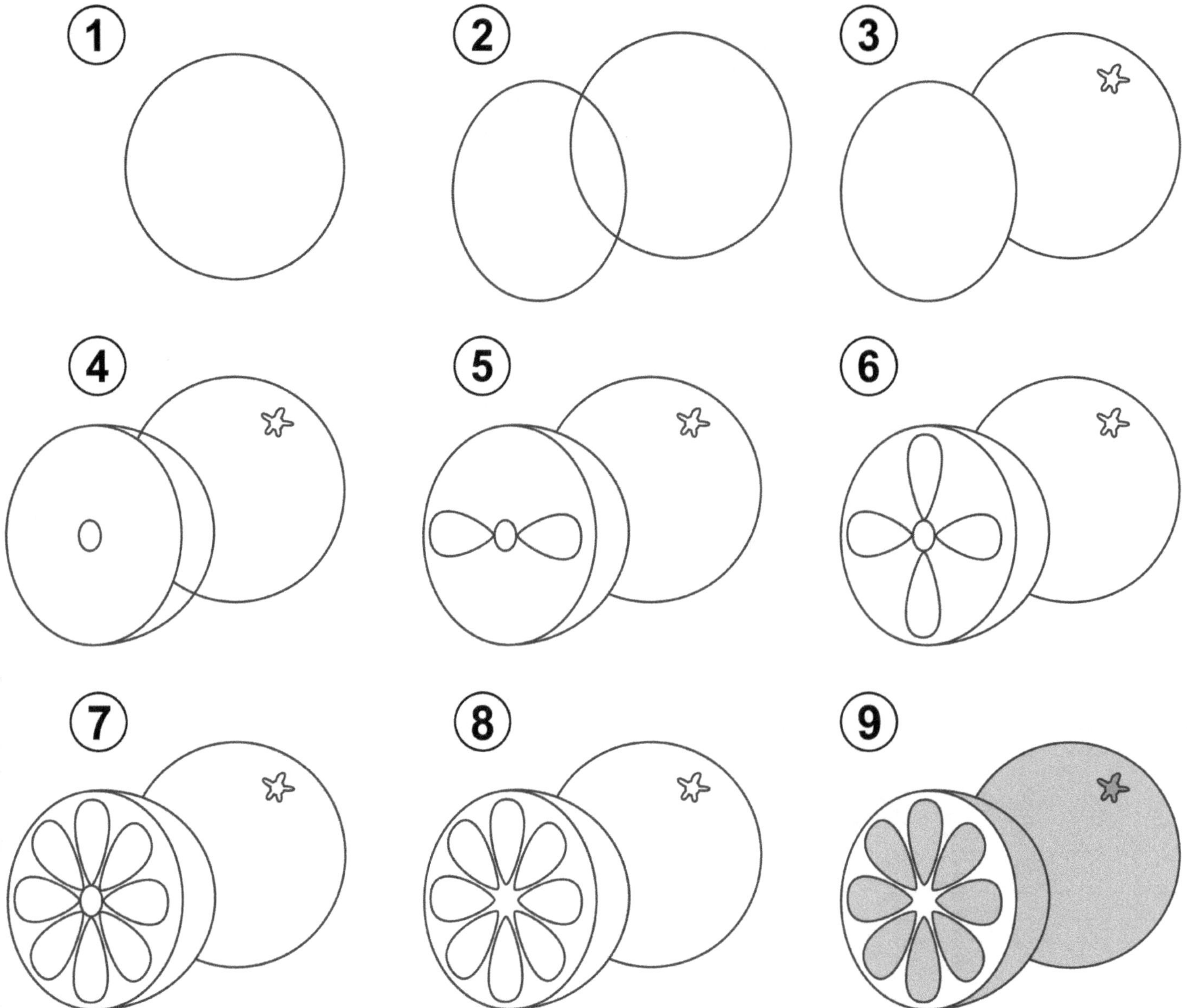

Your Turn to Draw

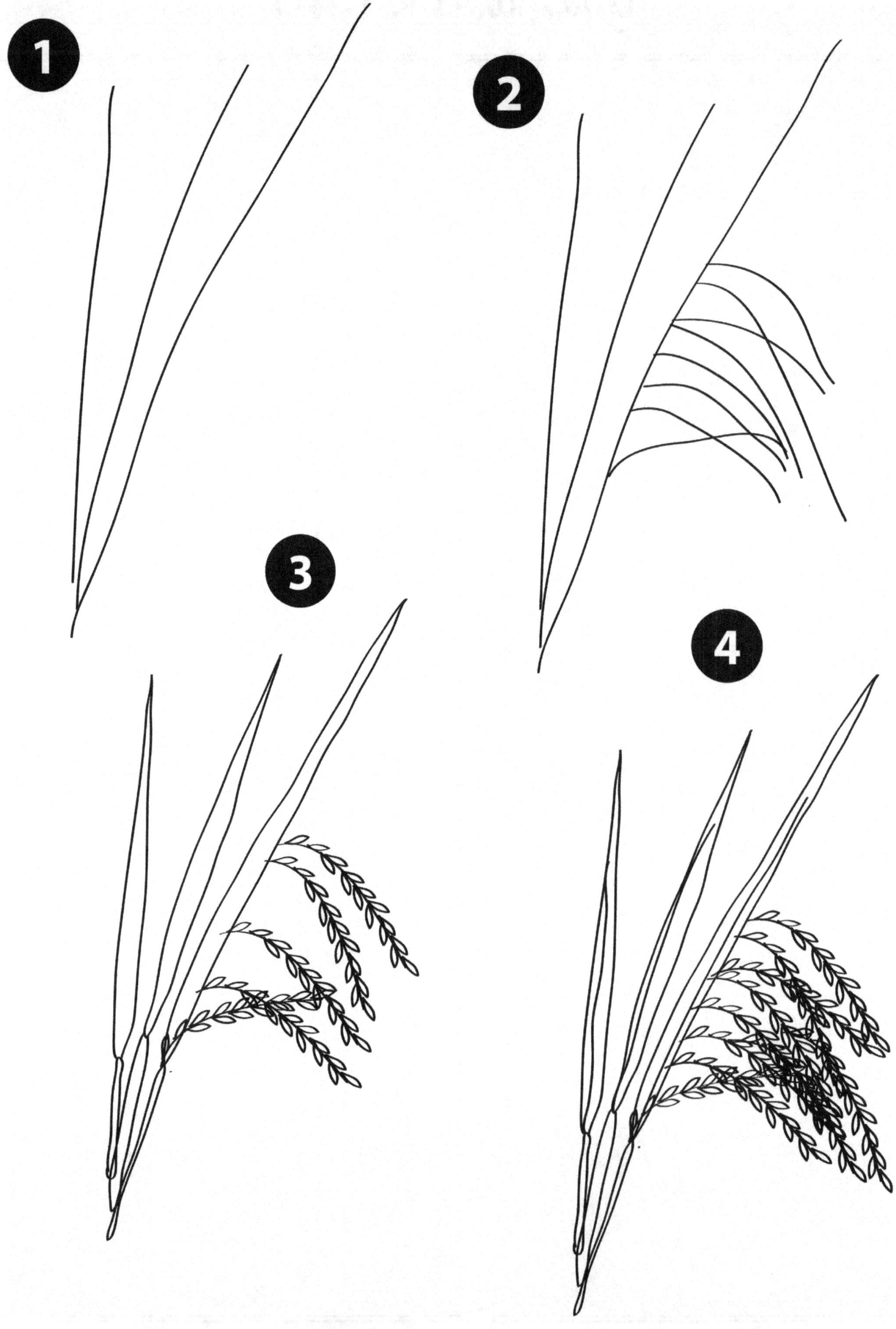

Your Turn to Draw

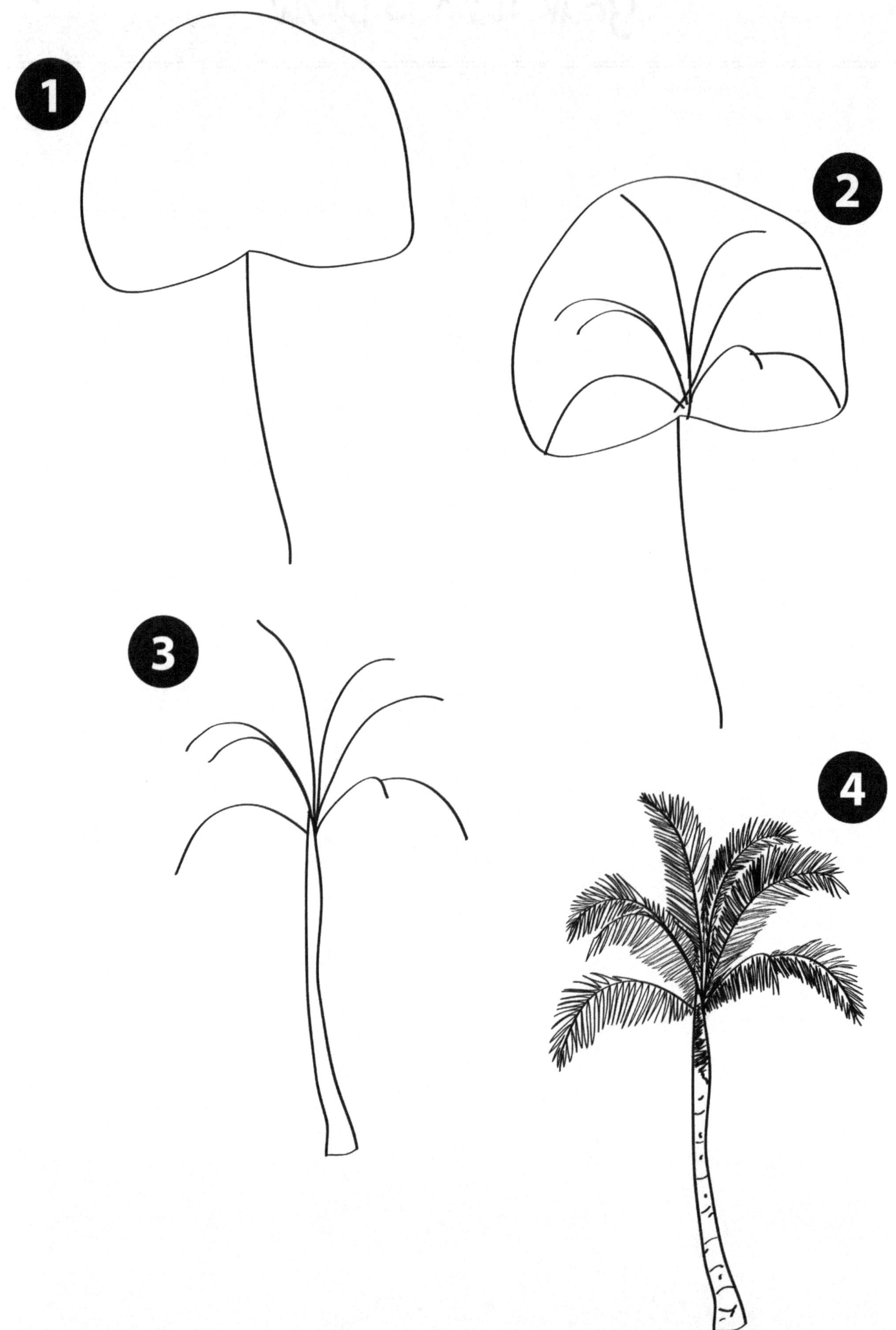

1
2
3
4

Your Turn to Draw

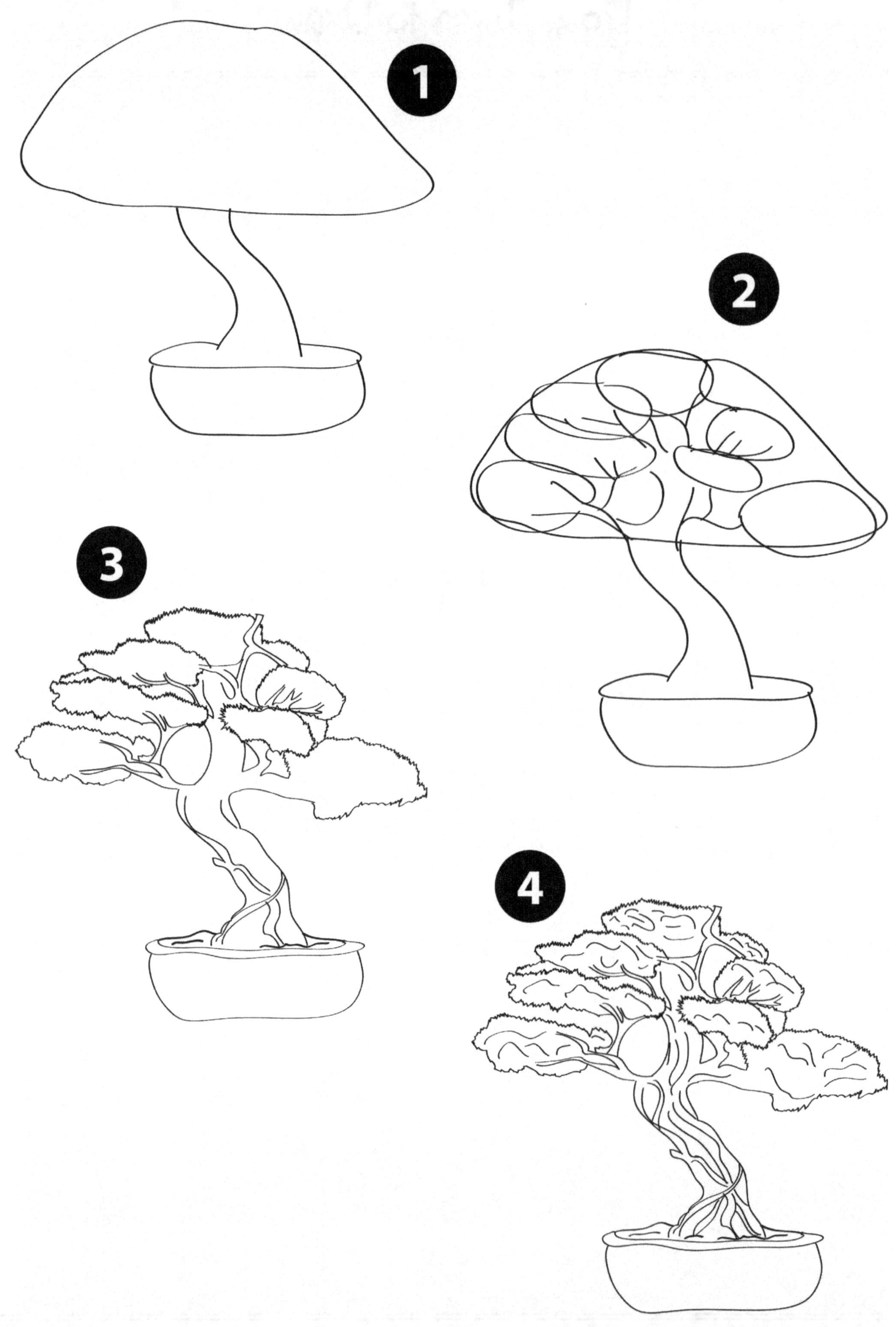

Your Turn to Draw

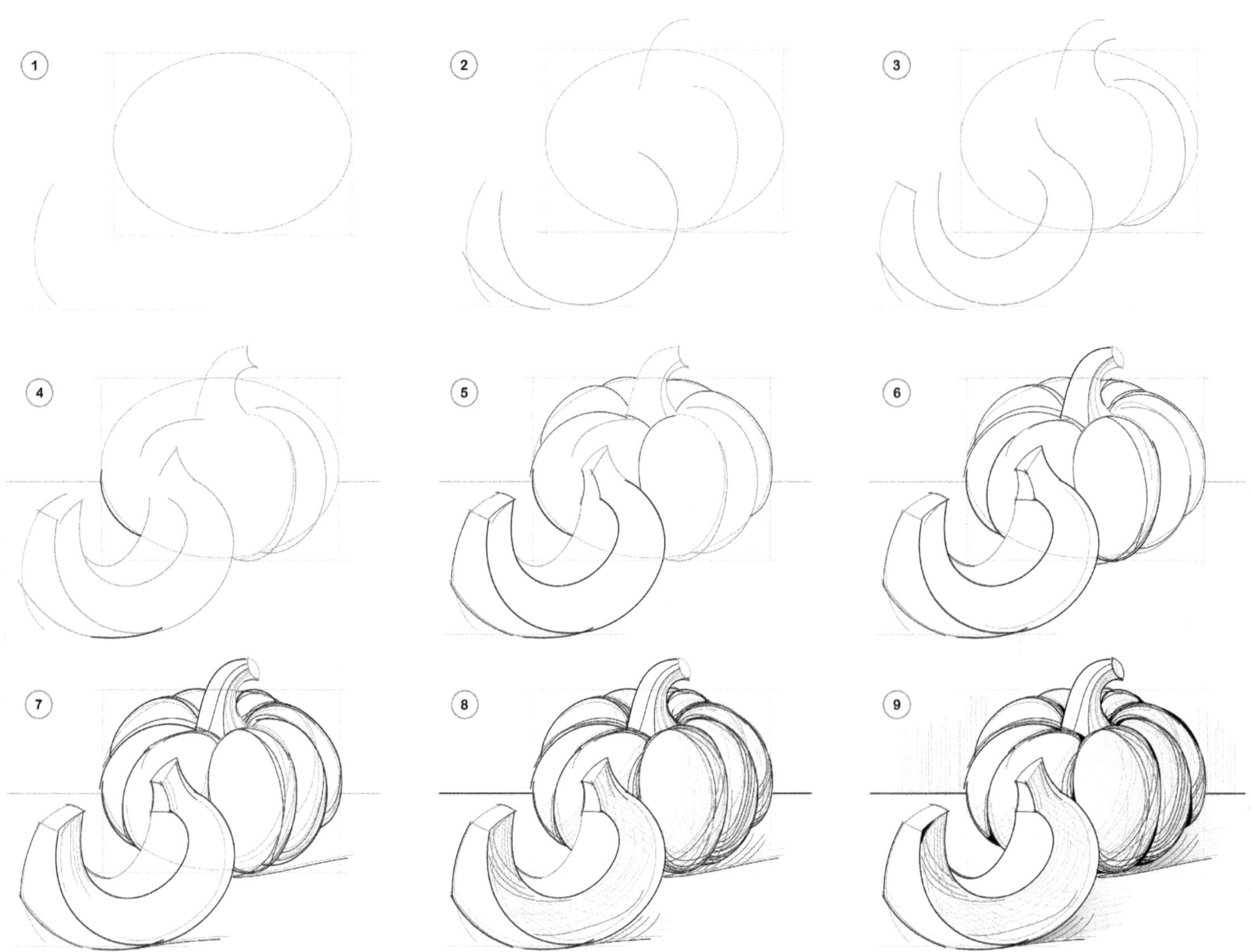

Your Turn to Draw

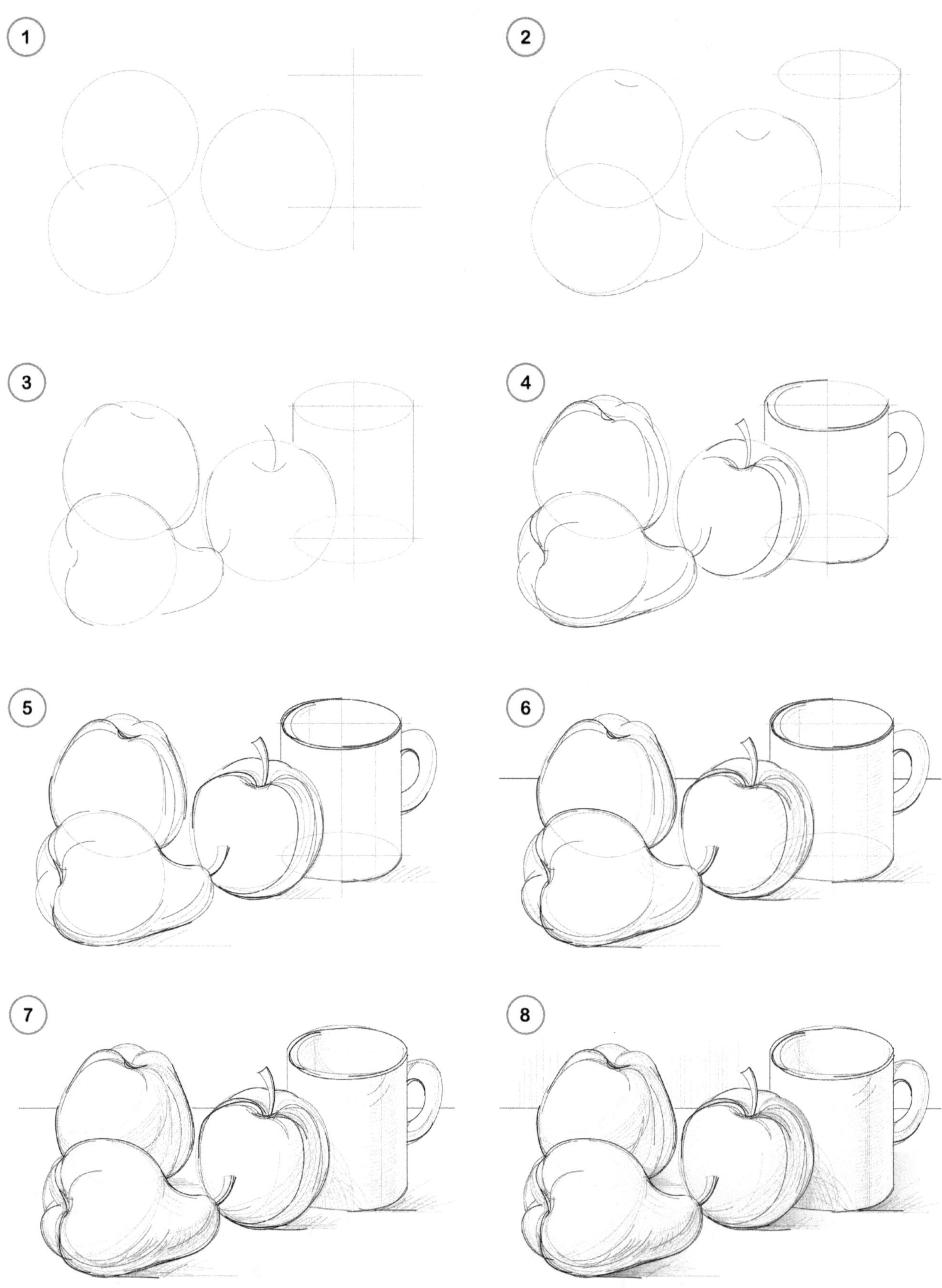

1
2
3
4
5
6
7
8

Your Turn to Draw

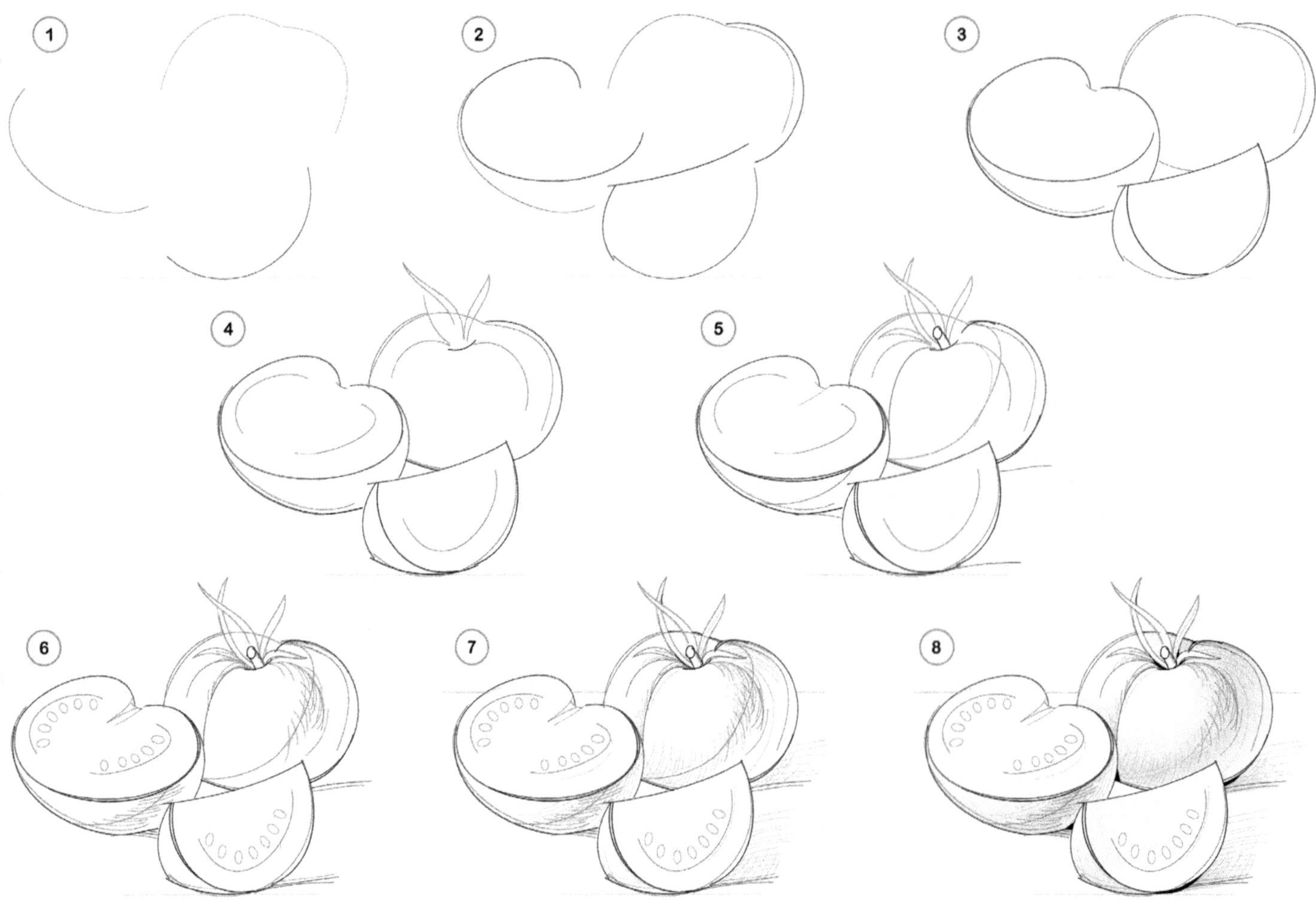

Your Turn to Draw

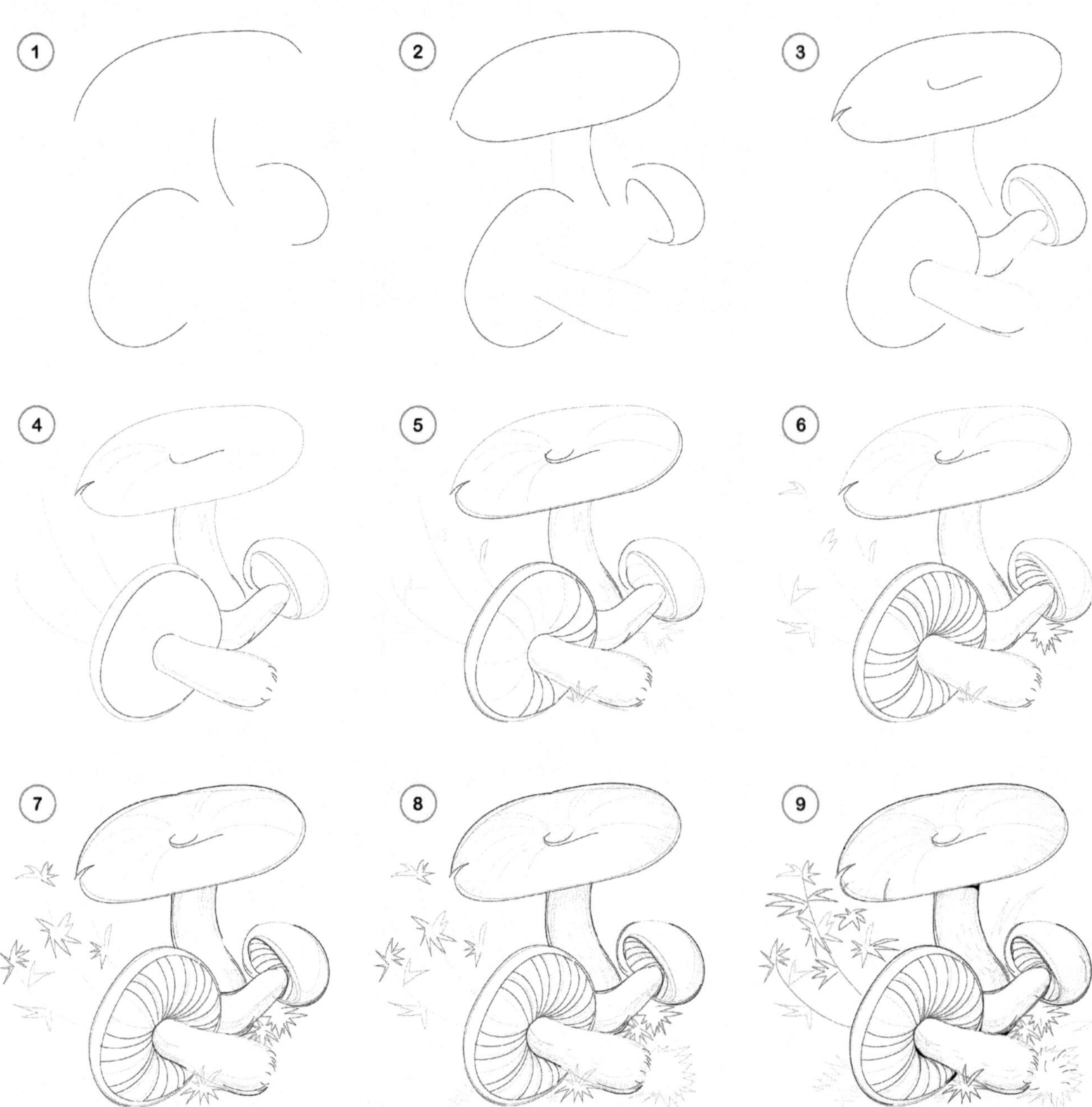

Your Turn to Draw

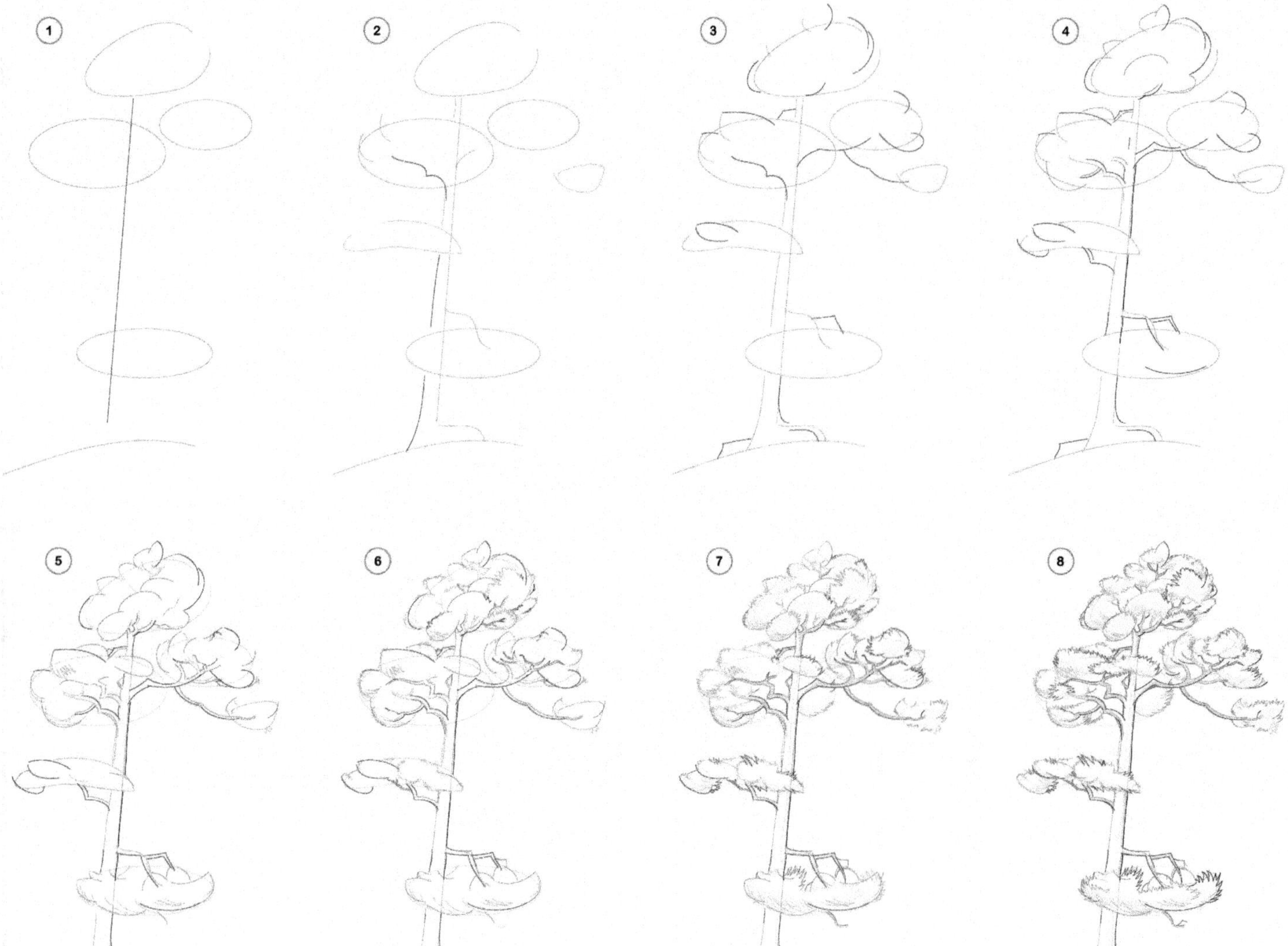

Your Turn to Draw

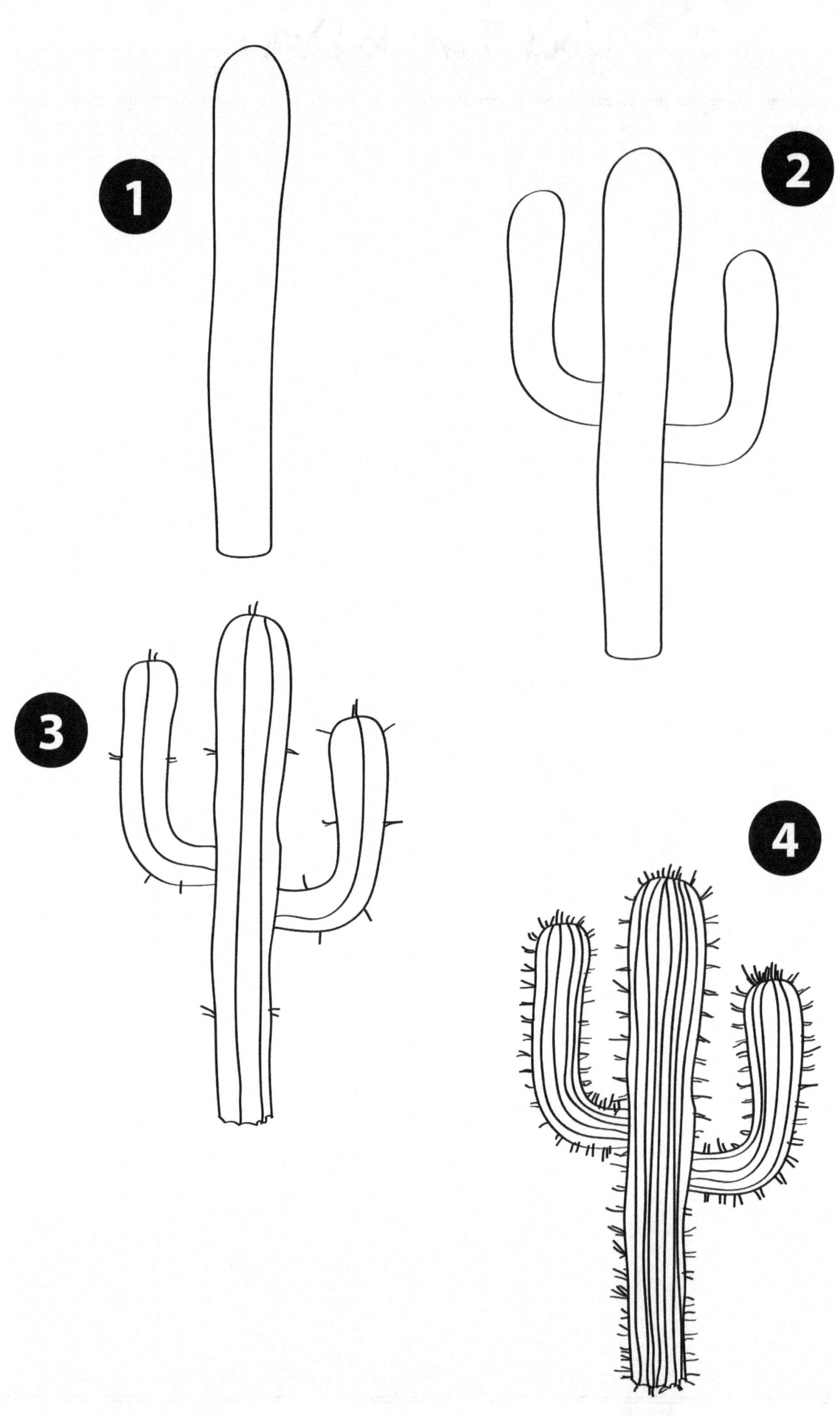

Your Turn to Draw

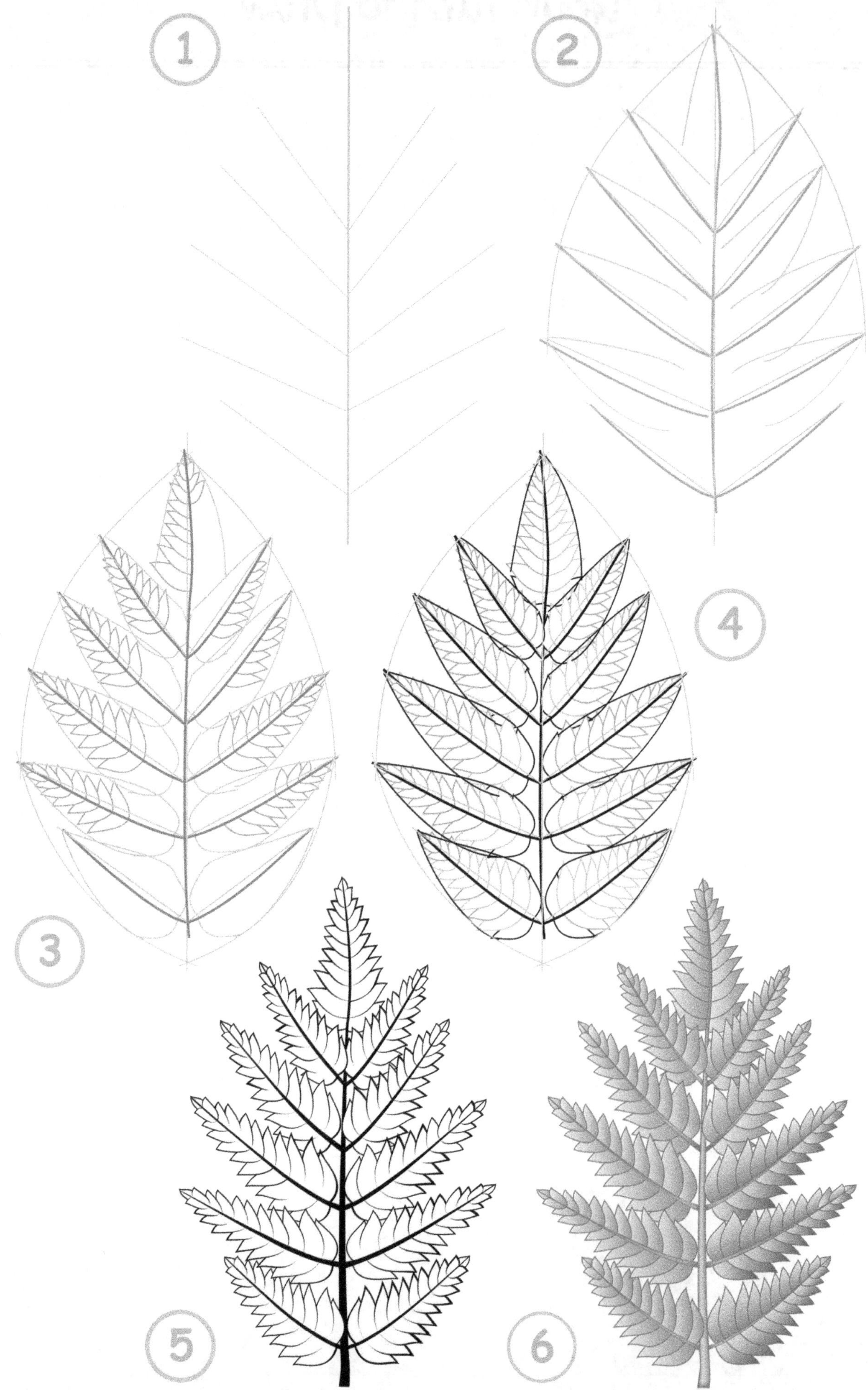

Your Turn to Draw

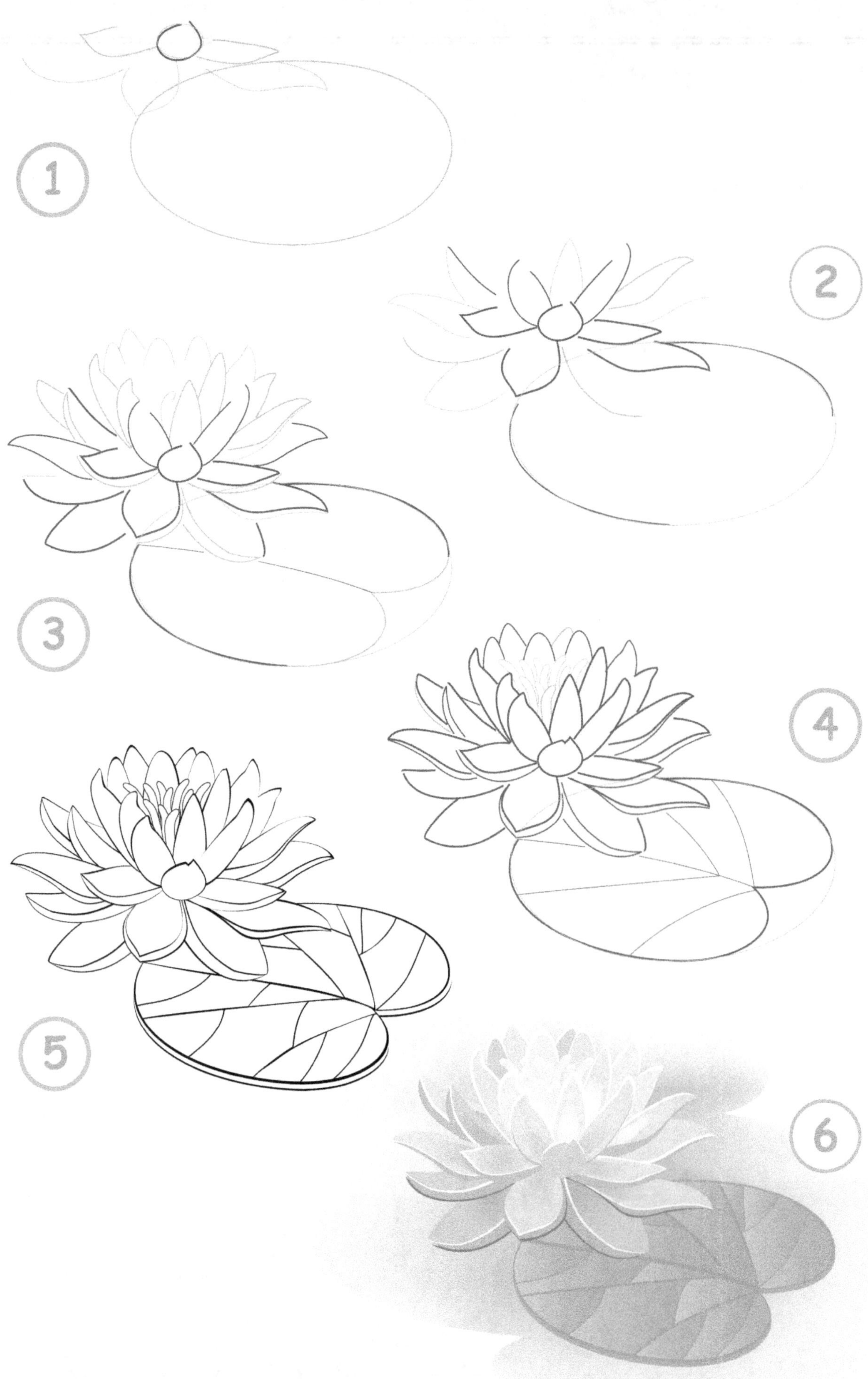

1
2
3
4
5
6

Your Turn to Draw

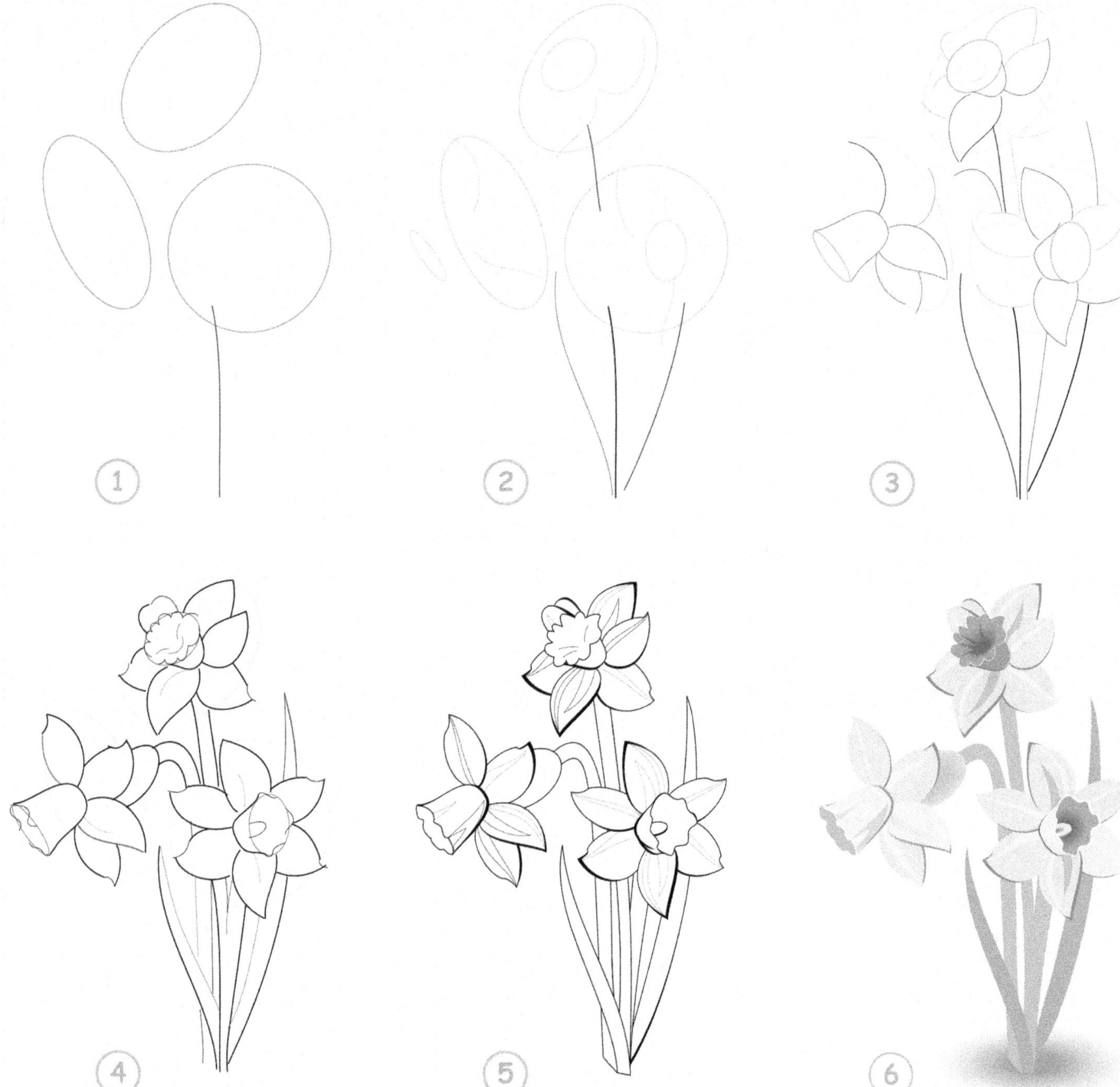

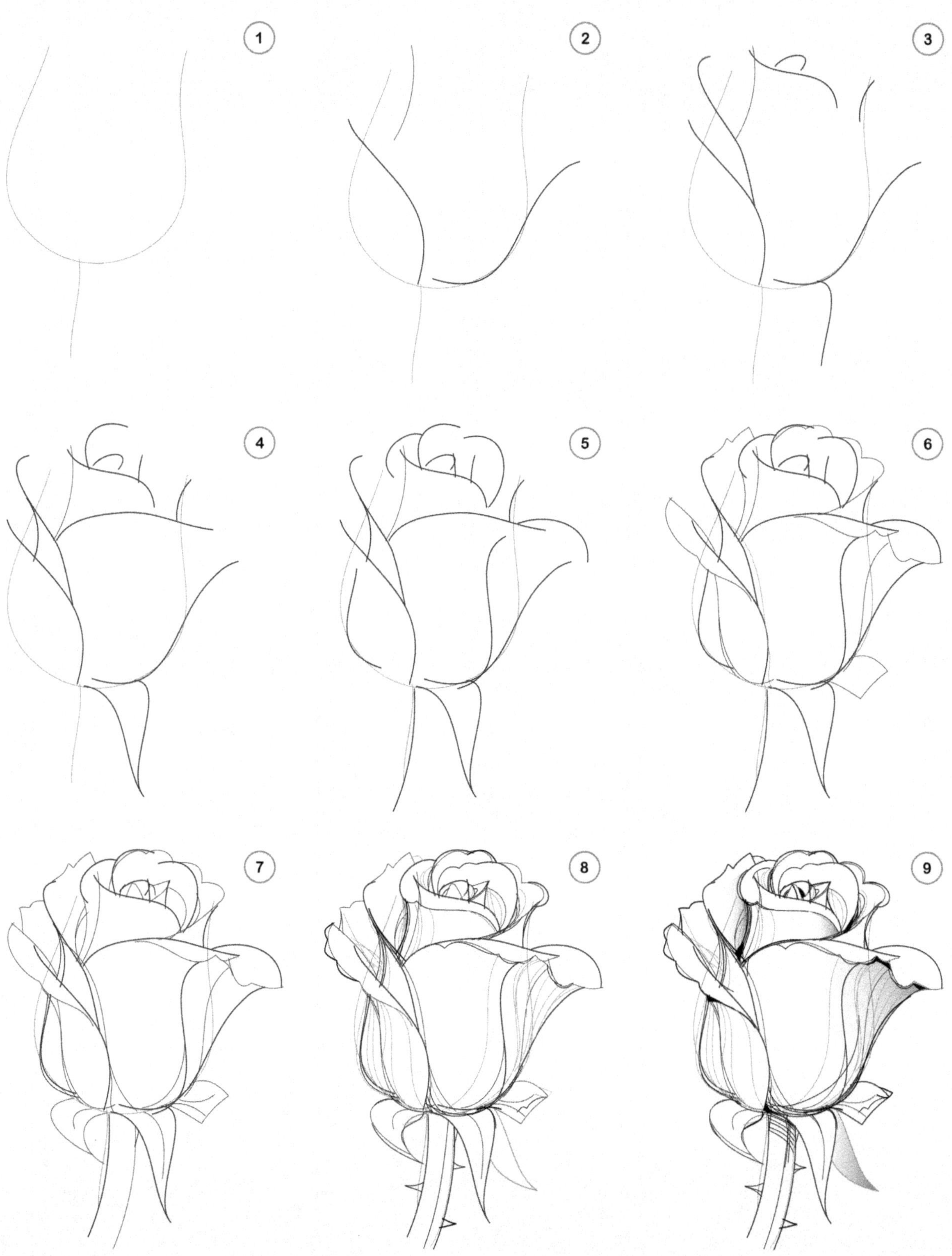

Your Turn to Draw

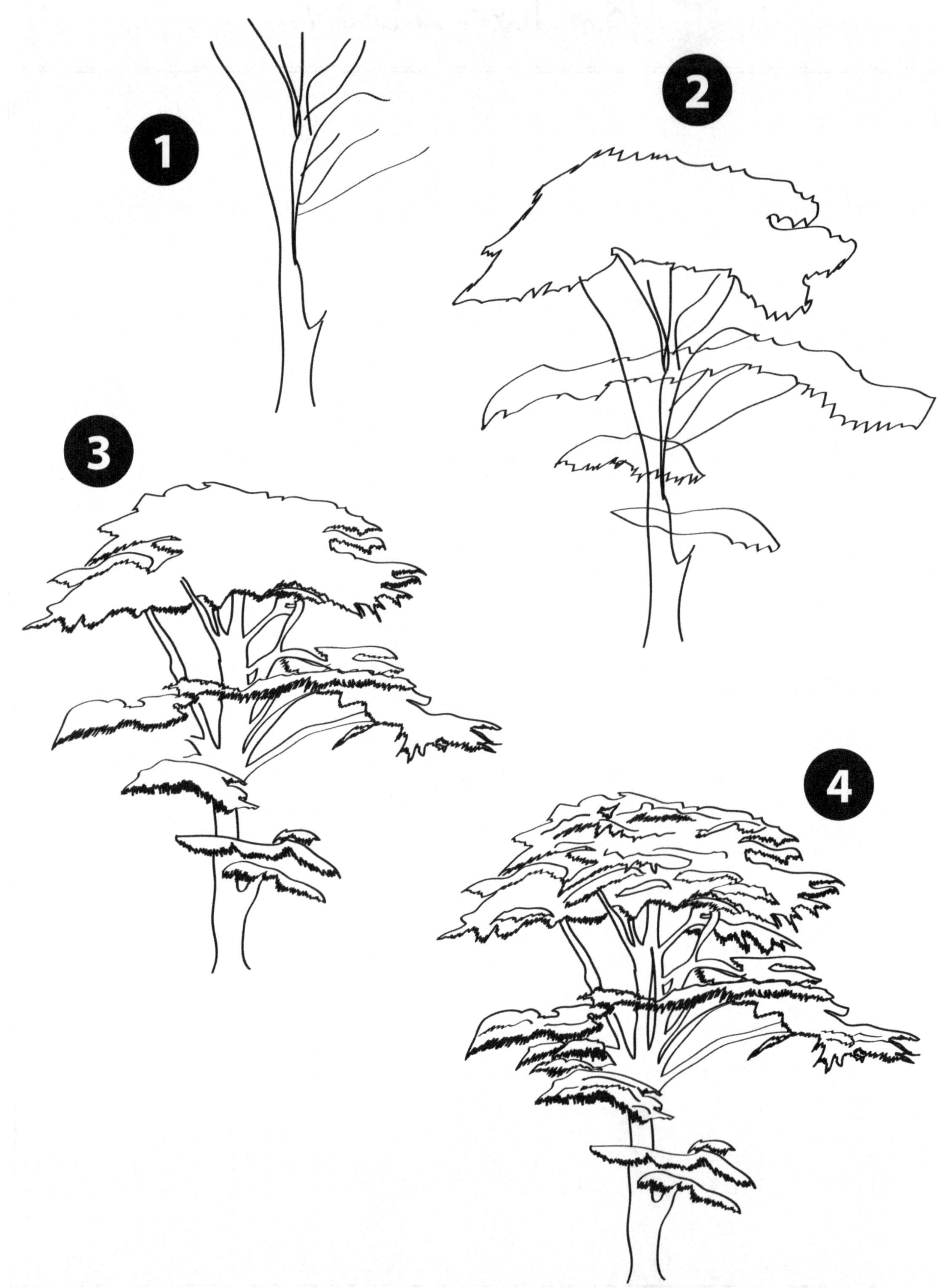

Your Turn to Draw